D0066041

The Vocation of
the Theologian

The Vocation of
the Theologian

Edited and with an Introduction
and Epilogue by
THEODORE W. JENNINGS, JR.

FORTRESS PRESS   PHILADELPHIA

Library of Congress Cataloging in Publication Data

Main entry under title:

The Vocation of the theologian.

   Contents: Theology as churchly reflection/Geoffrey Wainwright—The-
ology as holistic reflection upon the experience of women/Rosemary Radford
Ruether—Theology as critical reflection and liberating praxis/José Míguez-
Bonino—[etc.]
   1. Theology—Methodology—Addresses, essays, lectures.
I. Jennings, Theodore W.
BR118.V6 1985   230′.01   84–48722
ISBN 0–8006–1838–6

      1271I84   Printed in the United States of America   1–1838

Contents

The Contributors   vii

Introduction: The Crisis of Theology   1

1. Theology as Churchly Reflection   9
   Geoffrey Wainwright

2. Theology as Critique of and Emancipation from Sexism   25
   Rosemary Radford Ruether

3. Theology as Critical Reflection and Liberating Praxis   37
   José Míguez-Bonino

4. Theology as a Public Vocation   49
   Gordon D. Kaufman

5. Theology as the Construction of Doctrine   67
   Theodore W. Jennings, Jr.

6. Theology as the Interpretation of Faith for Church and World   87
   Langdon Gilkey

7. Theology as Thoughtful Response to the Divine Call   104
   John B. Cobb, Jr.

8. Theology as the Expression of God's Liberating Activity
   for the Poor   120
      James H. Cone

9. Theology as Reflection Upon the Roots of Christian
   Culture   135
      Thomas J. J. Altizer

Epilogue: The Vitality of Theology   143

Index   147

The Contributors

Geoffrey Wainwright is Professor of Systematic Theology at the
Divinity School of Duke University. His commitment to a liturgical theology is represented by his *Doxology: The Praise of God
in Worship, Doctrine, and Life* (1980).

Rosemary Radford Ruether is Georgia Harkness Professor of Theology at Garrett-Evangelical Theological Seminary. Dr. Ruether
is a Catholic theologian and historian whose work has contributed
to an understanding of eschatology, the relationship of Christianity and Judaism, and dimensions of feminist theology. Her most
recent book is *Sexism and God-Talk: Toward a Feminist Theology*
(1983).

José Míguez-Bonino is the director of postgraduate studies of the
Institute of Advanced Theological Studies in Buenos Aires and a
president of the World Council of Churches. He is widely known
as an interpreter of and contributor to Latin American liberation
theology (represented by his *Doing Theology in a Revolutionary
Situation* [1983]).

Gordon D. Kaufman is Mallinckrodt Professor of Divinity at Harvard
Divinity School. His most recent contribution to the clarification
of the meaning of the concept of God is to be found in *The
Theological Imagination: Constructing the Concept of God* (1981).

Theodore W. Jennings, Jr., is Research Associate Professor of Systematic Theology at the Candler School of Theology of Emory University and is also professor of theology at the Seminario Metodista de Mexico in Mexico City.

Langdon Gilkey is Shailer Matthews Professor of Theology in the Divinity School of the University of Chicago. A student of Reinhold Niebuhr and Paul Tillich, Dr. Gilkey expresses his concern for the relationship of theology to contemporary theology in many volumes, including *Naming the Whirlwind* (1969) and *Reaping the Whirlwind* (1977).

John B. Cobb, Jr., is Ingraham Professor of Theology at the School of Theology at Claremont and Avery Professor at the Claremont Graduate School in Claremont, California. Dr. Cobb is best known for his development of process theology as expressed in such books as *A Christian Natural Theology* (1965) and *Christ in a Pluralistic Age* (1975).

James H. Cone is Charles A. Briggs Professor of Systematic Theology at Union Theological Seminary in New York. Dr. Cone, founder and leading exponent of black theology, has given expression to his concern to ground North American theological reflection in the experience of oppression, struggle, and liberation of the black community in such works as *Black Theology and Black Power* (1969) and *God of the Oppressed* (1975).

Thomas J. J. Altizer is Professor of English at the State University of New York at Stony Brook. The subject of considerable controversy, Dr. Altizer is the leading voice in the "Death of God" debate of recent years and a student of Eastern religion and Western culture. Dr. Altizer's abiding concern to articulate a nonecclesial and biblical faith comes to most recent expression in *Total Presence* (1981).

Introduction:
The Crisis of Theology

Why the question of the vocation of the theologian? The essays in this volume grow out of the perception of a crisis in contemporary theology. This crisis is perhaps most evident in theology as an academic discipline within the university, but it is also present in the context of the school of theology, seminary, or divinity school which has long been the principal locus of theological work. The crisis is such that it prompts us to ask: What is it that theologians ought to be doing? What is the task of theology today? Is theology a possible task, and if it is, is it a fruitful or important task? In short, the crisis is a crisis of vocation for theologians and for those who would become theologians.

At first glance we might suppose that there is no such crisis, that theology and theologians are doing quite well. Institutions that call themselves divinity schools, theological seminaries, or schools of theology, and thus presumably are centers of theological interest and activity, appear to be reasonably healthy, training thousands of students and employing hundreds of faculty members many of whom even label themselves "systematic theologians." Doctor of Philosophy programs in "systematic theology" are more numerous today than in previous periods of our history and continue to attract large numbers of exceptionally well qualified students. Moreover, anyone who undertakes to survey the literature appearing annually in books and journals produced by academic theologians may be astonished and perhaps even overwhelmed by the sheer quantity of respectable scholarship generated by those who have committed themselves to the vocation of theology. On the surface, then, we see many signs of life and energy, of growth, and of apparently fruitful diversity.

Yet alongside this picture we may place another and a far more disturbing one. It is that of the deflection of theological energy, the avoidance of theological tasks, indeed, even the abdication of theological responsibility. Because it is this picture which has served as the impetus for the commissioning, collecting, and publication of these essays, it is important to attend to it with some care. We turn first to signs of crisis in theology considered as an academic discipline.

Perhaps the most striking feature of contemporary North American theology is its characteristic attention to questions of methodology and of the foundations of theological work. This scrupulous attention and unflagging concern make clear a determination to avoid wishful or sloppy thinking and a commitment to canons of scholarly integrity which makes nonsense of the popular impression of theologians as "doctrinaire," "dogmatic," or even, in the journalistic sense, "theological." No presupposition is left unexamined, no mode of argumentation taken for granted, no norm or source not subjected to the most critical scrutiny. I know of no other discipline in the humanities or in the sciences which is so committed to such a relentless and unwavering self-examination.

This commitment to methodological scrutiny is an indispensable component of theological inquiry. Understood in this way, the vast and growing literature in the field dealing with questions of hermeneutics and historicity, of epistemology and presuppositions, of language and meaning, may be a sign of health and vigor. But there is growing danger that the work of theology is being displaced by the work of preparing to do theology. Increasingly, questions of method take on a life of their own, absorbing the energy of theologians and endlessly deferring the work for which they claim to be laying the foundations or preparing the prolegomenon. The methodological preoccupation of North American theology may be in danger of becoming an obsessional neurosis.

If concern with theological method and questions of epistemology may be termed pre-theological, then we must add to this a post-theological preoccupation as a second sign of the crisis in contemporary theology. Much of the work of today's theologian, not only in scholarly writing but also in courses taught, focuses upon the recent history of theology. Indeed, from a reading of seminary cat-

alogues one would quickly gain the impression that systematic theology is a subfield of the history of theology. The historian, one
would gather, is concerned with all that occurred before Schleiermacher. But everything from Schleiermacher to liberation theology
belongs to the department of "systematic theology." This relegation
of theology to a historical subdiscipline is an astonishing development—all the more so as it appears to occur as a matter of course.
The result is that one gains the unmistakable impression that theology is something always already done by somebody else.

To be sure, the work of theology cannot proceed at all if one is
oblivious to the work of previous or contemporary theologians. Like
philosophy, theology is necessarily involved in critical attention to
its own tradition and is, moreover, a dialogical discipline which must
be conducted in conversation with other inquiring and critical minds.
Thus this "post-theological" inquiry is indispensable for constructive, systematic theological work. But it is not yet that work itself.
To the extent to which it succeeds in postponing or deflecting or
avoiding the work of constructive or systematic theology it becomes
self-stultifying, relegating itself to its own past. It then becomes a
sign not of lively conversation but of crisis.

A third sign of the malaise in academic theology is the proliferation
of what has been called a conjunctive theology: theology and psychology, theology and literature, theology and the social sciences,
and so on. Each of these conjunctives is accompanied by its own
body of scholarship and finds institutional form through the development of subfields, departments, sections in the Academy of Religion, and so on. These endeavors spring from the intention of
demonstrating the significance of theological work for other disciplines of the arts and sciences and from the indispensable desire to
learn from these other disciplines whatever they may have to contribute to a better understanding and prosecution of theological
tasks.

Unfortunately, however, what begins as a bridge may end up as
an island. That which seeks to connect two disciplines may succeed
only in becoming a third. The conjunction becomes an institution.
All too often the "theology" side of the conjunction is merely pre-
supposed and thus silenced. The result is a dialogue in which only
one voice speaks, hearing in reply only an echo. Then it is that

theologians desiring to attend to what, say, psychologists are saying band together to form a discipline in which they talk only to one another.

Careful and critical attention to its own presuppositions and method, a vigorous dialogue with its own tradition, and the proliferation of attempts to develop bridges to other disciplines in the arts and sciences may very well be signs of intellectual integrity and vitality. Certainly it would be folly to counsel an oblivion to troublesome epistemological issues, a forgetfulness of its own heritage, an isolation from the other disciplines of the university. There can be no question but that these activities not only may but also must continue to flourish within the field of systematic theology.

The crisis is to be seen not in these activities taken by themselves but in the way in which these activities have usurped the place of actual constructive and/or systematic theological work. It is only when this central and crucial work is being done that it becomes possible for theology to contribute anything of substance in its conversations with other disciplines. It is only when constructive theological proposals are actually made that the questions of presupposition and method take on pertinence and responses to these questions become persuasive. It is only when one takes on the work of theological construction that the contributions of other theologians may be accurately assessed and critically appreciated. In the absence of this constructive theological work, questions of method endlessly proliferate and only defer what they pretend to prepare. In the absence of theological reformulation, an interrogation of the work of other theologians can only be historical or journalistic in character. In the absence of real theological construction, our dialogue with other disciplines becomes an empty echo to which no one need pay any attention. It is the absence, lack, and silence at the center of our work which transforms our scholarly productivity into feverish busyness.

It is not only within the domain of academic theology that signs of this crisis appear. In the professional schools that take upon themselves the name of *theological* seminaries or schools of *theology* (divinity) and that have the task of educating the intellectual and professional leadership of Christian (and other) communities of faith, we may discover additional signs of this crisis. The most striking of these is the threatening rift between the historical, exegetical, and otherwise "scholarly" fields on the one hand and the practical, professional, and "experimental" fields on the other.

This tension and separation is one that closely concerns the work of the theologians, for it is the work of theology to provide a critical reflection upon ecclesial praxis and to translate historical inquiry into the reformulation of the language of contemporary faith. Where this work is not done, or is not done well, these professional schools are "theological" in name only. It then becomes difficult or impossible to justify the presence of "biblical studies" in the seminary rather than in departments of antiquities or Hellenistic studies. The history of the church and its doctrine appears as an intrusion from, or as a strange "double" to, the departments of medieval and modern institutional and intellectual history. On the other side, homiletics becomes communication theory and public speaking, liturgics an arcane preoccupation with quaint practices, and pastoral counseling an amalgam of therapeutic practices and theories unrelated to the intellectual and ethical claims of anything worthy of the name of practical or applied *theology*.

To the extent to which anything like the situation I have been describing exists in contemporary American seminaries or schools of theology it must be blamed, not on the intellectualism of historians and exegetes nor the anti-intellectualism of homileticians and pastoral counselors, but on the abdication of responsibility on the part of theologians. For it is the systematic theologians themselves who have increasingly turned their discipline into an adjunct of the history of doctrine, claiming for themselves "everything since Schleiermacher" while at the same time in their own work failing to attend carefully to the work of exegesis and history. This can most certainly not be blamed upon the exegetes and the historians. Similarly, it is systematic theology which has withdrawn its attention from the language and practice of the community of faith and turned to a preoccupation with the language and practice of other theologians.

Other observers of the work of systematic theology may paint a picture that is somewhat different from the one I have just sketched, identifying the crisis in theological vocation in varying ways. Yet most would agree that the discipline has been undergoing a crisis. It was on account of this generally shared sense that the faculty of the School of Theology and the Graduate Division of Religion at Emory University undertook to redesign the graduate program in systematic theology. We sought to design a program responsive to this crisis, one that would encourage our students to undertake the task, responsibilities, and challenges of constructive and systematic theology. As a part of this work, it was agreed to invite a number of distinguished theologians to Emory not only to consult with us about the design of the graduate program but to speak on the topic "The Vocation of the Theologian." The essays gathered in this volume grow out of this consultation.

These essays are concerned not with the crisis in theology but with the vocation of the theologian. They do not seek to bemoan the present situation but seek to chart the way forward and to summon others and encourage one another to undertake the tasks, accept the responsibilities, and heed the challenges of systematic constructive theological work. The theologians who have written these essays share a common commitment to what may be termed constructive theological work. That is, in addition to the important methodological and historical work that many of them have done, they have contributed to the constructive reformulation of particular doctrines or matters of theological substance. They are concerned in various ways with the dialogue between theology and other disciplines, other religions, and other cultural and political movements. Yet, above all, they are concerned with these matters as theologians, as persons who have accepted the responsibility for the critical reformulation of Christian doctrine and praxis.

The essays by José Míguez-Bonino, Gordon D. Kaufman, John B. Cobb, Jr., Langdon Gilkey, and Geoffrey Wainwright were delivered at Emory. The essays by Thomas J. J. Altizer, Theodore W. Jennings, Jr., and Rosemary Radford Ruether were commissioned for this volume. James H. Cone was prevented by the press of other responsibilities from preparing a new essay for this volume. His views, which are important both for our consultation and for this volume, are represented here by an earlier essay. The editor is grateful to him and to Clark Williamson, the editor of *Encounter*, for permission to republish Cone's essay "What Is Christian Theology?" (here titled "Theology as the Expression of God's Liberating Activity for the Poor").

It has been by no means possible to include in this volume all the perspectives that would be important for an understanding of the work of theology today. However, it has been our purpose not to provide a typology of theological perspectives but to provoke further discussion concerning the challenges and responsibilities of theological work in our time and setting.

To the theologians who have contributed essays to this volume the editor expresses profound appreciation. Similarly, the faculty of the Graduate Division of Religion and of the Candler School of Theology made this volume possible by the liveliness of their interest in, and discussion of, this topic. Without the generosity and vision of Jim L. Waits, the Dean of the School of Theology, the consultation would not have been held, the papers written, the volume edited. To him therefore both I and the other contributors to this volume and, indeed, all those who find this discussion helpful owe a great debt of gratitude.

Theodore W. Jennings, Jr.

1
Theology as Churchly Reflection

GEOFFREY WAINWRIGHT

Existential Perspectives

If you invite a theologian to talk about "the theologian's vocation," you are inevitably asking for a certain amount of autobiography. I will try to make the autobiography subserve what may be called the existential perspectives. As will in any case become apparent later, the individuality of the theologian is irreducibly part of the theological enterprise.

To begin geopolitically. As an undergraduate at Cambridge, I had a mind to enter the British colonial service. By the late 1950s, however, the Empire was shrinking rapidly, and it became evident that there was no scope for a full career in its service. At the level of general providence, one might say that by the events of the *Weltgeschichte*, God was clearing the way for me to become a theologian. At the level of particular providence, a more positive preparation was taking place. For my bachelor's degree I studied modern and medieval languages, in particular French and German. Not only has linguistic facility given me direct access to the most formative theological writings of continental Europe, my studies in European history, philosophy, literature, and art opened up the area in which the most sustained interplay has occurred between the Christian faith and human culture—and the relationship of "Christ and culture," to use H. Richard Niebuhr's phrase, has been a constant theme in my own theological thinking. More grist came to that mill during my six years, from 1967 to 1973, as professor of systematics at the Protestant Faculty of Theology in Yaoundé, Cameroon—a newly independent country with its own interesting spot in African ethnology and having recently been administered first by Germany as a colony and then by France and Britain under United Nations mandate. After that partial fulfillment of earlier tropical dreams, I returned with a keen eye to Britain and taught for six years at Queen's College in Birmingham, an Anglican and Methodist seminary. That return to roots provided, I think, a certain stability and sustenance that have stood me in good stead since my move in 1979 to New York and to Union Theological Seminary, an apocalyptic city of violence and high achievement and an academic institution whose sympathy for radical-liberal causes often runs counter to the traditional orthodoxy of my own beliefs.*

But I have jumped ahead. I do not imagine that I would have become a professional theologian had I not heard a call to the ordained ministry. University Christianity was very much alive in the 1950s. Coming from a Methodist family, I had been active in the Cambridge University Methodist Society ever since going up to the university in 1957. One bright summer's morning in 1959, during Arnold Morris's sermon at Wesley Church by Christ's Pieces, I suddenly knew that I had to become a Methodist minister. I started to preach, and from 1960 to 1964 I studied theology, first at Cambridge after completing my B.A. and then at Wesley College, Leeds. I served as a probationer minister in the Liverpool South circuit when the Beatles were at the height of their fame and then was ordained in 1967. My ministerial mentors had encouraged me in an academic direction, and I managed to put in time over the years at the University of Geneva (through the Ecumenical Institute at Bossey) and at the Waldensian Faculty of Theology in Rome. My book *Eucharist and Eschatology* (1971) gained the doctorate at Geneva (1969). Ministry and theology have always been close together in my experience. While in the pastoral ministry in Liverpool, I wrote my book on *Christian Initiation* (published in 1969). While teaching systematic theology in Yaoundé, I acted as minister in the English-speaking church of a French-speaking city. At Queen's College in Birmingham we were busy in chapel and in spiritual direction, and I shared in Methodist ministerial life at the circuit, district, and connectional levels.

Again, let me go back and broaden this personal account to include

---

*Since the delivery of this paper, Professor Wainwright moved again—to become Professor of Systematic Theology at Duke Divinity School. —Ed.

the more general ecclesiastical and theological scene as I have observed it and played a part in it. In the late 1950s and early 1960s, three movements reached their classical form, at least in Britain and continental Europe, and my initial perceptions were strongly shaped by them: the biblical movement, the liturgical movement, and the ecumenical movement. The Scriptures, not understood fundamentalistically but nevertheless taken as the Word of God, have actively remained for me the primary source of faith and theology. I enjoyed teaching some Bible for a couple of years in Birmingham, and my sermons are almost always governed by the lectionary readings. After the heyday of biblical theology, scriptural scholarship went through some lean years. But I now find encouragement in the trend eminently represented by Brevard Childs's *Introduction to the Old Testament as Scripture* (1979), while in New Testament, Raymond Brown, my former colleague at Union, is not ashamed to treat the Bible as a religious book.

The Bible's living location is the worship of the church. The attraction that the liturgical movement held for me was in part aesthetic: I am a cricket fanatic, now converted to baseball, and I love to think of the liturgy, with Jean-Jacques von Allmen, as "an eschatological game." The aesthetic aspects of worship receive a spiritual and mystical transcendence that is quite palpable in the liturgy of the Orthodox churches, where I find renewal from time to time. The sacramental density of worship is important to me in all churches, and it is always disappointing to see Methodist churches failing to recover the high sacramentalism of the Wesleys.

Thanks to the ecumenical movement, our own deficiencies can find some remedy, but only if we are prepared to pray and work for the unity of Christ's church. Through my teacher Raymond George I was early introduced to the World Council of Churches, and I remain committed to the classic Faith and Order goal of organic unity in which different traditions will continue to affect us at the level of spirituality but in which denominations as such will have no structural place. My ecumenical vision is basically "multilateral," even though circumstances may temporarily demand closer attention to some "bilateral" relationships. In England I share the English Methodist love-hate relationship with the Anglican Church, where social and cultural factors play a much larger part than the abstractly theological; and (or but!) I am quite convinced that significant ecumenism in England is possible only with the Church of England as a full participant. I see the current proposals for covenanting among the several English churches, on which I worked for four years in the Churches' Unity Commission, as only a step on the way toward more complete unity. My most sustained bilateral relationships have probably been with Roman Catholicism, dating from the exciting days of Vatican II—with occasional and irregular intercommunion at the local level, membership of official bilateral teams, reading acquaintance with the theological giants of the senior generation (Yves Congar, Karl Rahner, Edward Schillebeeckx), and personal colleagueship with those nearer my own age (Walter Kasper, Nicholas Lash, Jean Tillard). My latest bilateral experience has been with the Lutherans, who in this country seem to find some sympathetic features in my theology (there have been few Lutherans in places where I have lived hitherto). At the moment, I tend to look on Lutheranism as a necessary critical irritant whose function is to prevent the rest of Christendom from exaggerating the grain of truth that is undoubtedly present in Pelagianism. In World Council of Churches circles I have developed friendships particularly with Wolfhart Pannenberg from West Germany and Ulrich Kühn and Martin Seils from East Germany.

In talking of the theologian's vocation, I have up to now been talking of *this* theologian's vocation, how it came and how it has so far worked itself out. That was a way of concretizing two constituent connections of theology, two of the existential perspectives that are indispensable to it: namely, faith and the church. Let the pendulum now swing to the most objective part of this discussion. One way of defining the nature of theology is to compare and contrast it with one of its nearest neighbors on the broader intellectual front, namely, religious studies. The issue may be formulated in terms of scientific status.

Scientific Status

The thesis, which would eventually become even more refined in its nuances if more time were available, may at the outset be boldly stated thus: Religious studies must be scientific; theology can only be confessional.

While the institutional history of the Western world leaves us with many mixed cases (of which the Candler School and Emory University is one), it may nowadays be said that the typical location of religious studies is the secular university or college, while the typical location of (Christian) theology is the church college or seminary. Let us look first at the position of religious studies in the secular university. Purely from a phenomenological point of view, religion can impose itself as a proper object of study: first, it is a widespread, if not universal, feature of human life; second, religions play a prominent part in the lives of their adherents; and, finally, religions make serious claims to truth. But what kind of study is appropriate? Academic study requires congruity with what, according to the best lights of the time, is considered "knowledge"; it is also pursued in the expectation that it will make an addition to such knowledge. Now the dominant model for knowledge in the West, since the nth century, has been the natural scientific, whose persuasiveness has been reinforced by the achievements of its technical application. How can religious studies (and theology insofar as it includes them while surpassing them, as I will argue) "measure up" (the image is significant)? The hard sciences, archetypical of what Stephen Toulmin[1] calls "compact disciplines," make these demands:

1. They demand objectivity. The student is to be governed by the object studied. That is proper, and indeed necessary, for religious studies too, and even for theology, as Karl Barth and then T. F. Torrance argued in their revelational way. Granted that constructive interpretation is part of scientific work, the hypothesis always remains subject to challenge by "things as they are." There is, however, a more fundamental connection than the one between objective reality and explicatory hypothesis; and this fact is important for the scientific status of religious studies and theology. I refer to the connection between observer and observed. At least since Werner Heisenberg, the natural sciences have known that to observe is to affect the situation. Natural scientists tend to look on this fact as a regrettable necessity, which one must somehow try to correct. The human sciences, including religious studies, have on the whole made more positive use of "participant observation" (in various modes) as a method: the look which is both critical and sympathetic engages the student as a human being. In theology,

there is no knowledge of God without love of God; and that means an acknowledgment of God's sovereignty to judge us who "study" him. Could it be, in any case, that participation is a necessary route to knowledge?

2. The hard sciences proceed by measurement and calculation. A certain empiricism is not out of place in religious studies, or even in theology—especially in reference to a religion of creation and incarnation, where revelation and salvation are concretely mediated. But the transcendent God, who remains "immense" and "free," finally evades measurement and calculation. Theology will not be contained within positivistic limits, and even religious studies will have to beware of reductionistic accounts that fail to do justice to the claimed experience of believers.

3. The hard sciences demand that claims to knowledge be testable by the community of competent scholars. The idea of competence begs several questions, but some such notion is necessary also in religious studies and theology. In the case of theology, however, scholarship is not the only test. The theologian is accountable also to fellow believers and even to the pastoral and doctrinal authorities of the church. Theologians may of course assert their intellectual freedom over against ecclesiastical authority, and sometimes perhaps the cause of truth has been advanced in that way; only, they must expect to forfeit, at least temporarily, the benefits of an official role, and in extreme cases even membership, in the church. Talk of academic freedom in a secular libertarian sense is quite beside the point in the case of a would-be Christian theology.

In discussing scientific criteria, we have found that the natural sciences do not provide a watertight model for the human sciences (including religious studies), let alone for theology. Closer neighbors in the university are more likely to be found among Toulmin's "diffuse", "would-be" or even "quasi" disciplines: sociology and psychology (which often fight for their own scientific status on naturalistic terms but which are never value free, as the natural sciences at least ideally are), history (where particular views of "the human project" are always implied), literature and the arts (where engagement and response are the only way into the reality being studied). These "disciplines" may have to fight for their places in the university over against an imperialistic natural-scientific conception of knowledge, especially when the latter is supported by technology and politics. Religious studies, and theology where it happens to have a place in the university, may have to join the struggle on the humanistic side, pleading the importance of religion in human experience and society. The theologian will, however, scent a danger here—that of "the civil religion," with its loss of the particular in favor of the most generally acceptable. We thereby come to theology proper.

Theology (I mean here Christian theology; one could, no doubt, say at least some similar things, *mutatis mutandis*, in connection with theology done in the context of another religion[2]) is most typically located in a church institution. One might now attempt to distinguish between theology and religious studies in a way proposed by David Tracy. Whereas religious studies are concerned with meaning only, theology is concerned with meaning *and truth*.[3] Again, this statement needs to be nuanced. For the explication of *meaning*— which requires the process of translation into another frame of reference—already implicitly raises the question of truth. It is in theology that the matter of truth becomes explicit. But what is more precisely the nature of theology's concern with truth? Does one only have to look for truth—or must one be persuaded that one possesses, or is possessed by, the truth in order to "do theology"? Despite the dangers (and theology is a risky occupation), the latter is the case. Karl Barth's image was that faith is indispensable to the theologian, be his faith no bigger than a mustard seed.[4] As I see it, there is no point in wanting to annex all serious concern for truth into the area of "theology." To be doing theology, it is not enough to be addressing "God-shaped questions," or, in Brian Hebblethwaite's more sophisticated phrase, to reckon with the possibility of "an ultimate horizon of meaning."[5] Philosophy is an honorable name for that way of looking at things. You can even call it the philosophy of religion. But *theology* presupposes that there are "God-shaped answers," or at least a notion, as Pannenberg puts it, of an "all-determining reality" which may be called God.[6] John Updike somewhere likened philosophy and theology to a ceaseless process of knitting, unraveling, and knitting up again. That may be so for philosophy. But the Christian faith believes that there are some constant, irreversible God-givens, which the theologian is not free to undo. By that I do not deny that interpretation of the inheritance is necessary in changing cultural contexts, and that in such a process of interpretation the truth of the tradition is put at stake. Nor, of course, can one stop criticism of particular versions of the faith, but to be engaged in such criticism is not necessarily to be doing theology.

None of this absolves the theologian from respecting, in an appropriate way, the procedures of the human sciences, and even of the natural sciences; but it certainly means that the theological disciplines have broader and deeper dimensions than those disciplines which are methodologically atheistic. Thus scriptural scholars will use the tools of archaeology and philology: the incarnational principle is the theological justification for seeking to know what happened and how things were understood. Scriptural scholars will not, however, treat the Bible just as an ancient text, but rather as the book of the church which informs a living liturgical and spiritual tradition in which they themselves participate. Exegesis and hermeneutics are inseparable. Again, church historians will investigate the past as accurately as possible and will probably in our culture have to respect the particular canons of post-Enlightenment historiography by avoiding naively interventionistic accounts of the acts of God in history. But they will also have to respect at least the interpretations given by believing participants in significant moments of church history (that much is allowed by William A. Clebsch in his *Christianity in European History*[7])—*and*, if they have even an ounce of prophetic soul in them, they will seek to discern in faith the concursive operation of God in, with, and under the people, events, and movements of human history (for if God is not believed to be actively present at least in that way, then the Christian game is not worth the candle, as Bultmann himself recognized). Biblical scholars and church historians are themselves theologians in the ways I have suggested. Their work is taken up into the most integrative form of theology, which is systematic theology. And to that we now turn as the very epitome of the theologian's vocation.

Systematic Theology

In theology, as in all human existence and study, there is need for comprehensive vision. Otherwise, as George Steiner says, we "constrain the life of understanding to fragments of reciprocal irony or isolation."[8] Systematic theology, or more concretely *a* systematic theology, is the attempt by a believer to describe, in an intellectually coherent and responsible way, the *entire* Christian faith from a *particular angle*. Its scope is as comprehensive as the creeds themselves, stretching from "God the Father almighty, maker of heaven and earth" to "the resurrection of the dead and the life of the world to come." Yet the standpoint of every systematician is limited by time and space and by the systematician's own individuality. A certain pluralism is thereby both inevitable and proper in *theology*, but it must remain the Christian *faith* which the theologian is trying to describe; a test of the theologian's fidelity and adequacy in this respect will be the reception accorded to the theologian's attempt, in both the shorter and the longer term, by other Christian believers and perhaps by the doctrinal authorities in the church and the churches. Historical and geographical circumstances allow and require a certain cultural concreteness in any systematic theology ("contextuality" is the slogan); but it is not the business of a systematic theology to give detailed refutation to any currently fashionable form of antireligious philosophy (that is the affair of apologists), to supply exhaustive guidance in the face of contemporary moral dilemmas (that is for ethicists to engage in), or to pronounce instant evaluations concerning ephemeral political excitements (that is a job for journalists). Theological monographs on individual themes remain necessary, but I would have little respect for would-be systematicians who went on confining themselves to occasional pieces that remained mere *Stückwerke*, without at least an implied coherence of the parts in a comprehensive whole.

How, then, is a particular systematic theology to be judged? Judgment can be fairly made only by a person or a group of people who themselves take up a consistent stance and are ready to propose, if necessary, a coherent alternative vision. It cannot fairly be done by sniping from a floating platform. Granted those conditions, the appreciation of a systematic theology can be undertaken in the light of the following questions. How, and in what interrelationships, does the theologian use his or her material sources: Scripture, tradition, human experience? What kinds of reasoning does she employ? How does his work stand with regard to the best available knowledge in his time and place? How is her work structured, and in what relationships do the parts stand to each other and to the whole? From what particular perspective, and with what dominant interest, has the author written? To whom is his work addressed, and with what purpose? What practical effects would the adoption of her vision have in regard to the coming of God's kingdom? How and where is the author open to correction and development from the wider church, from the future, and even (insofar as God is interested in our theologies) from God?

All thinking Christians tend toward the construction of a theological system, however implicitly. But it is perhaps only to those who are vocationally charged with making their system public that such a formidable array of questions should be put. As one who has tried to fulfill that burden, I may perhaps be allowed to state one or two considerations that I would like borne in mind when my own work is evaluated. A few words, then, about my doxological approach.[9]

Doxological Approach

Purely pragmatically, most Christians are born and nourished in the faith through the worship of the church, and most church members perceive the ordained minister as, above all, the leader of the church's worship. The corresponding theological truth is that liturgy, along with evangelism and loving service, is a constitutive activity of the church. Properly understood, worship is indeed the ultimate raison d'être of the church: "Man's chief end is to glorify God, and to enjoy him for ever" (Westminster Shorter Catechism). There is an Eastern Orthodox dictum that "the true theologian is the person who prays";[10] and in the liturgies of St. Mark and St. Basil the doxologies addressed to God at the Sanctus are called "theologies."

Certainly my own Christian perceptions have been decisively shaped by the hymns of the Wesleys, and it is there that I continue to find the "proportion of the faith." (How sad I am that this has so often to be done in private these days, because the American *Hymnal* contains so few Wesleyan hymns, and even the new British hymnal will reduce their number compared with the rather generous 1933 *Methodist Hymn Book*). In any case, I have always been attracted to the liturgical perspective in theological reflection, because it is in the worship of the church that I have best caught the Christian vision. And my most influential teachers have been those whose examples, in one way or another, have encouraged me in that direction: Raymond George (British Methodist), Nikos Nissiotis (Greek Orthodox), Franz J. Leenhardt and Jean-Jacques von Allmen (Swiss Reformed). In my book *Doxology* I have unfolded that approach more amply than I know of its being done elsewhere in recent times. I do not, of course, consider that the result in that particular book is the only possible result of adopting the liturgical perspective. To the contrary, I hope that many other theologians will produce their own pictures from that broad angle. Nor do I claim that the liturgical perspective is the only appropriate one for theology. The other two constitutive activities of the church—evangelism and loving service—call for the adoption of the missionary and ethical perspectives. But just as I have tried to include questions of witness and morals in my liturgical perspective, so I would expect the missionary approach to include cult and conduct, and the ethical approach to include worship and witness.

You will not have missed the ecclesiological reference in all I have been saying. The doing of theology is inescapably individual: just as the act and attitude of faith require personal commitment, so we cannot avoid personal accountability in theological reflection upon the faith. But the doing of theology, though individual, is not individualistic. The believer-theologian lives and works within the fellowship of the church, draws sustenance from the church, and seeks to serve the church—which is itself in the service of God, who is himself in the service of the world, seeking its redemption. Hence the theologian, by helping to clarify the church's vision, contributes at least indirectly to the church's proclamation and so to the salvation of the world.

Having ventured to publish a comprehensive systematic theology, I am inevitably faced by the question, What next? One possibility would be to work in more detail on some parts of a picture that had on the whole been painted in rather bold strokes. And I may eventually come round to further special work on Christology and on the doctrine of the Trinity. But for the moment, I have chosen a different procedure for my next long-term project. In *Doxology* I wrote straight from the dogmatic heart of Christianity. Now I want to undertake a sustained treatment of the relationships between theology and the disciplines that neighbor it at its human end. Far from abandoning the doxological character of theology which I have advocated and practiced, based as it is on the belief that God is the origin, strength, and goal of theology, I aim to show how a doxological approach may illuminate other human endeavors and the study of them. And here I want to acknowledge how much I appreciate the work of some theologians now at Emory. On the epistemological and hermeneutical side, I value Professor Jennings's early book, *Introduction to Theology: An Invitation to Reflection Upon the Christian Mythos*;[11] and I have been fascinated by his recent article "On Ritual Knowledge."[12] In aesthetics I look to Professor Saliers for illumination.[13] If my rather ambitious project can be brought to a conclusion, we may end up with something like a theological anthropology.

So much for my own plans. But let me now try to list some outstanding questions to which at least some among the theological community ought to be devoting their energies, as indeed they already are. Naturally we shall work ecumenically, as an indirect contribution toward Christian unity. And I take it for granted that direct work will continue on the doctrinal reconciliation of the churches.

Outstanding Questions

Let me locate the issues on three geographical levels: the whole world, the first world, and the new world.

On the global scale, there is, first of all, the question of the religions. What are the proper relationships of Christ, of the Christian faith, of the Christian religion, to the great religions of the world? Ease of travel and of communication forces this question upon us from all directions, with a breadth that the church has never previously had to face. There is much work to be done in "religious studies"; but from the theologian's viewpoint, that work is but a preliminary, albeit a necessary preliminary, to the strictly theological question, How do other religions appear in the light of the Christian faith? Years of practical acquaintance and sustained dialogue will be necessary. And we must tread delicately, for our theological interlocutors in other faiths believe, too, that truth resides with them; and our perceptions are sometimes mutually contradictory. Premature conclusions are to be avoided; but one's instinct of faith is likely to point in certain approximate directions while refusing others. My sense is to refuse both a Barthian exclusivism and John Hick's "Copernican revolution," whereby God replaces Christ at the center, while Christianity becomes a circling planet among others.[14] But I do not yet see anybody ready with a satisfactory positive account of the matter.

The second global question is that of earthly stewardship, in both its ecological and its economic aspects: the husbanding of material resources and their just distribution. It is the preacher's job to rouse Christians to reflection and action on these issues. The theologian's task is to clarify the protological, soteriological, and eschatological dimensions. As the Eastern Orthodox fathers especially point out, the vocation of the human creature includes a royal priesthood on behalf of the cosmos, to rule it in God's name and to offer it to God in praise. The human vocation includes also a communal life marked by justice and indeed by love, as both Old and New Testaments make plain. The goods of the earth are a sign of God's bounty, and our sharing of them is a qualitative test of our gratitude. Yet, "man does not live by bread alone"; and although Christians must heed the critique that the hope of heaven has been used to divert the economically oppressed from the task of revolutionary change on earth, we cannot curtail the Christian message without being guilty of another robbery. Among sensitive Marxists there are hints of a hunger for transcendence, both in respect of grace (called forth by human failure) and in respect of eternity (because of the persistency of death). In this second area of global questions, I resonate very much with Professor Runyon's article, "The World as the Original Sacrament,"[15] and I have been intrigued by his essay that juxtaposes Marx and Wesley on human work and Christian works.[16]

The third global question is that of peace. Again, the theologian has the responsibility of clarifying issues from faith's perspective. Last year in the Soviet Union I gave a long interview to a correspondent of the Tass news agency. He wanted to talk of peace. I knew I would not make the front page of *Pravda* as soon as I spoke of humanity's fall away from the living God and the self-destructive tendency thereby acquired; and of earthly peace needing to be grounded in the reconciliation which God offers human beings with himself. In this matter we need to steer between activism and quietism. On the one hand, we need to remember that if our present generation were to destroy the earth today or tomorrow, God has already through the centuries built up quite a community of saints with whom to enjoy eternity. On the other hand, we have the responsibility of giving the best earthly shape we can to the values of God's kingdom, and peace is certainly one of those values.

Let us scale down now to the first world in particular. The main theological question facing the Western world, North Atlantic "Christendom," is the question of secularity. Old hat, you say? Have we not left the 1960s behind? Let me confess that I never engaged very heavily with the so-called secular theology of that decade—either because I was astonished at the intellectual and spiritual feebleness which could not see that a book such as Paul van Buren's *The Secular Meaning of the Gospel* represented the abandonment of the Christian faith, or because for part of the time I was residing in still religious Africa. The embarrassing naivetés of the 1960s inevitably provoked a reaction whereby in the 1970s Christian intellectuals could afford to be religious again. But the theological issue raised by aggressive or casual secularism has not gone away. The "plausibility structures" (to use Peter Berger's term) of large tracts of modern Western culture are indeed positivistic. And that, on the side of the world, sets the current terms of the perennial hermeneutical question: how to give a sufficiently intelligible account of the Christian faith as the basis for persuasive advocacy of a gospel message that will challenge the people in their unbelief. A certain pluralism of expression may be in order, but by no means "everything goes." I do not think we get anywhere at all by offering a deistic or unitarian account of God and a psilanthropic account of Christ.[17]

We come finally to the new world, more precisely to the United States. Now that I have lived in this country for three years, my best judgment is that Christian theologians here must navigate between two perils. On the one side stands the phenomenon of what Richard Hofstadter called *Anti-Intellectualism in American Life*. On the other side is the kind of Enlightenment rationalism exemplified

by book reviewers in *The New York Times*. The theological counterparts are fundamentalism and reductionism. We must seek to be
neither conservative nor liberal (I would refuse those two quasi-
political terms for talking about theology); our aim must, rather, be
a theology which is both intelligent and traditional. A living tradition
interacts intelligently with its environment in such a way as to renew
itself without forfeiting its historic identity. While with Jonathan
Edwards the American vision of a new world still took a Christian
eschatological form, the degeneration of the new into the merely
novel has brought the need to stress the Christian inheritance rather
than its cultural adaptation. It is with this emphasis that I wish to
see systematic theologians in this country go about what David Tracy
calls their hermeneutical task of explicating the Christian classic. I
believe that there are enough catholically and evangelically minded
Christians in the United States for them to produce a few theologians
who could contribute to the genuine renewal of Christianity here
and throughout the world.

NOTES

1. Stephen Toulmin, *Human Understanding*, The Collective Use and
Evolution of Concepts, vol. 1 (Princeton, N.J.: Princeton University Press,
1972).

2. I think of the first Gifford Lectures to be given by a Muslim: Seyyed
Hossein Nasr, *Knowledge and the Sacred* (New York: Crossroad Publishing
Co., 1982).

3. David Tracy, *The Analogical Imagination: Christian Theology and the
Culture of Pluralism* (New York: Crossroad Publishing Co., 1981), 20.

4. Karl Barth, *Evangelical Theology: An Introduction* (New York: Holt,
Rinehart & Winston, 1963), chap. 9.

5. Brian L. Hebblethwaite, *The Problems of Theology* (Cambridge: Cambridge University Press, 1980), 6f.

6. Wolfhart Pannenberg, *Theology and the Philosophy of Science* (Philadelphia: Westminster Press, 1976), chap. 5. Insofar as reality is still in-
complete, Pannenberg holds, God retains the scientifically appropriate
character of a "hypothesis."

7. William A. Clebsch, *Christianity in European History* (New York:
Oxford University Press, 1979).

8. George Steiner, *On Difficulty, and Other Essays* (New York: Oxford
University Press, 1978).

9. My "systematic theology" is set forth in my book *Doxology: The Praise*

of God in Worship, Doctrine, and Life (New York: Oxford University Press, 1980). Briefer statements may be found in my articles "In praise of God," *Worship,* 1979/6 (cf. 1981/5), and "Towards God," *Union Seminary Quarterly Review,* Inaugural Addresses, 1981.

10. Nilus of Ancyra (really Evagrius of Pontus), *On Prayer* 60 (J. P. Migne, ed., *Patrologia Graeca,* vol. 79, 1180): "If you are a theologian, you will truly pray; and if you truly pray, you are a theologian." And Evagrius of Pontus (Wilhelm Bousset, *Apophthegmata* [Tübingen, 1923], 309f.): "The Lord's breast is the knowledge of God, and whoever leans on it will be *theologos.*" It is not by chance that in the East, Saint John is called "the Theologian."

11. Theodore W. Jennings, Jr., *Introduction to Theology: An Invitation to Reflection Upon the Christian Mythos* (Philadelphia: Fortress Press, 1976).

12. Theodore W. Jennings, Jr., "On Ritual Knowledge," *The Journal of Religion* 62, no. 2 (April 1982): 111-27.

13. Several articles by Donald E. Saliers are to be found in *Worship* (1974/4; 1975/5; 1978/6; 1981/4).

14. John H. Hick, *God and the Universe of Faiths* (London: Macmillan & Co., 1973).

15. Theodore Runyon, "The World as the Original Sacrament," *Worship* 1980/6.

16. In Theodore Runyon, ed., *Sanctification and Liberation: Liberation Theologies in Light of the Wesleyan Tradition* (Nashville: Abingdon Press, 1981).

17. I rejoice in the recovery of trinitarian themes among the recent writings of German theologians: Karl Rahner, Walter Kasper, Gerhard Ebeling, Eberhard Jüngel, Wolfhart Pannenberg, Jürgen Moltmann. In this country the Lutheran Robert W. Jenson has published *The Triune Identity: God According to the Gospel* (Philadelphia: Fortress Press, 1982).

2
Theology as Critique of and Emancipation from Sexism

ROSEMARY RADFORD RUETHER

In theory, the vocation of a theologian should be the same for a man or a woman. However, in practice, at this time in the history of the Christian churches, one must speak of the specific vocation of a woman theologian in the general context of the vocation of a theologian. This is because, for most of their two-thousand-year history, the Christian churches have not only kept women from the ordained ministry, they have also kept women from the study of theology and from the public role of theologian in the church. Indeed, proscriptions against women as official teachers in the church are earlier and continue to be more vociferous than proscriptions against ordination. This is partly due to the fact that ordination was generally thought to be out of the question, while the possibility that the very real religious gifts of women might be perceived as giving them status as official teachers was continually seen as a threat to be averted. Thus one finds already in the post-Pauline strata of the New Testament the proscription of women as teachers:

> I permit no woman to teach or to have authority over men; she is to keep silent. (1 Tim. 2:12)

This ban against women as teachers or preachers is continued in the early church orders, such as the *Didascalia* (early third century) and the *Apostolic Constitutions* (late fourth century). The *Constitutions* declare that Jesus chose to commission men, and not women, and also that the male is the head of the woman, and conclude that, for these reasons, the woman may not be allowed to be in a position of teacher. This viewpoint is reiterated throughout the Middle Ages and is renewed in the Protestant Reformation in the mainline Protestant traditions. It continues to be echoed in nineteenth- and twentieth-century arguments about women's right to preach. Although a few theological schools, such as Oberlin College, were open to women in the nineteenth century, generally speaking, theological schools have been slower to admit women than other professional schools, such as schools of law or medicine. Harvard Divinity School admitted women to degree programs for the first time only in 1955, and many Roman Catholic seminaries still refuse to admit women today.

Feminist theologians are only beginning to glimpse the extent of the distortion in theological culture that has resulted from this long history of exclusion of women as theologians. First of all, women's experience was eliminated for the most part from the shaping of the official theological culture. That half of the human race that gestates, bears, and suckles children, whose body and psyche are subtly attuned to different rhythms and ways of perception of the world, was not allowed to enter into the conversation about God and humanity, good and evil, from her own perspective. Not only did this exclusion of women prevent women themselves from becoming theological learners and teachers, it also meant that theology was biased against them. The theological culture, both consciously and unconsciously, was pervaded by dictates that rationalized and justified women's exclusion by defining woman as an irrational and morally inferior expression of the human species unfit to learn, teach, and minister. Maleness and male experience were assumed to be the generic and universal expression of humanity as such, and the female was mentioned at all only to define her as the "other."

Many examples of this overt bias against women in the theological tradition can be cited. Augustine declares in his treatise on the Trinity that the woman lacks the image of God in herself, and is in the image of God only "when taken together with the male who is her head." Thomas Aquinas, following Aristotle, defines woman as a "misbegotten male" who is a defective or imperfect expression of human nature. Women are regarded as deficient physically, morally, and mentally. Physically, they are weak. Morally, they lack full capacity for control over their appetites and self-discipline. Mentally, they have less capacity for rationality. Because of this defective nature, woman cannot represent normative humanity. Only the male can represent headship or leadership, both in society and in the church. Aquinas also deduces from this that the maleness of Christ is not merely a historical accident, but is an ontological necessity. In order to represent the fullness of the human species, Christ must be incarnated into normative humanity: the male. It follows, then, that only males can represent Christ as priest. Such masculinist theology still lurks underneath the assertion in the 1976 Declaration of the Vatican against women's ordination that there must be a "physical resemblance between the priest and Christ."

The Reformation brought modifications, but no essential change, in this male view of theological anthropology. Luther draws from the mystical and monastic traditions in suggesting that Eve, in the original creation, would have been Adam's equal. But woman of the present is not the daughter of that original Eve, but of the fallen Eve, who has lost that original high estate and has been put by God into subjugation to the male as punishment for her sin. The subordination of woman is an expression of divine justice, and woman would be in rebellion against God as well as man to complain against it. By contrast, the Calvinist tradition follows Augustine in believing that female subordination is part of the original order of creation. As such, it mirrors the covenantal ordering of God over creation which is reflected in the human, social hierarchies of male over female, parents over children, and masters over servants.

The female theologian thus attempts to stand within and interpret a tradition that has been profoundly biased against her. This is possible only through a fundamental act of faith. This act of faith is not, first of all, in the church, the tradition, or Scripture. It is an act of faith or trust in God/ess; in authentic reality or in truth itself. This act of faith is in the fullness of woman's humanity and in a divine and created reality that intends and promotes that full humanity of woman. Whatever denies, diminishes, and distorts the full humanity of woman must be evaluated as nonredemptive. Theologically, this means that whatever diminishes or denies the full humanity of woman must be recognized as not reflecting the divine or authentic relation to the divine, nor the authentic nature of things, nor the message or work of an authentic redeemer or community of redemption.

This critical principle implies a positive principle. What does promote the full humanity of woman is of the Holy, does reflect true relation to the divine, is the authentic message of the Redeemer and the true mission of the community of redemption. We do not fully know what this fullness of woman's humanity means or can mean. Because it has been fundamentally distorted in history, one has only fragmentary glimpses of it. To affirm it is itself an act of faith in the true ground of our being over against all that has distorted and alienated us from our authentic humanity, and hence from each other, creation, and God/ess.

This critical and affirmative principle then becomes the norm for judging the tradition, including the Scriptures. One can stand within this tradition and claim to be renewing it only if this principle is, at the deepest level, the true principle of the Scriptures and tradition as well, in spite of all distortion by the sin of sexism. If this is not the true principle of the biblical and Christian tradition, then this tradition itself must be evaluated to be irredeemable and must be transcended by a new vision that would include woman fully. This is the position taken by Mary Daly and others of the Goddess or post-Christian spirituality movement. They become theologians for a new religion of woman which is in the process of being revealed.

If, however, one claims that the biblical tradition, despite all distortion, nevertheless does intend the full humanity of woman as created and redeemed, then this norm becomes a revolutionary one within the tradition itself. Both the Scriptures and the mainline traditions of Judaism and of Orthodox, Catholic, and Protestant Christianities must be seen as profoundly apostate from their own root principles insofar as they have been distorted throughout by a patriarchal social system.

There are three fundamental aspects or moments in this process of critical reflection on the theological tradition for the feminist theologian. The first moment of feminist theology is necessarily a critical or destructive one. It takes the form of unmasking the sexist bias of the biblical and theological tradition. Feminist scholars of Scripture and theology document this bias in various writers and periods of the tradition. General histories of sexism in theology are written, tracing this bias in the Scriptures, the church fathers, medieval, Reformation, and modern theologians. These more general accounts may be followed by more in-depth accounts of particular eras and persons, showing the complex nuances of this bias against women. This, in turn, enables the general story to be told with greater accuracy and subtlety, but without losing the clear critical issues in the maze of detail. There emerges from this critical work a recognition that the androcentric bias of the tradition is not accidental or superficial. It is not the expression of the idiosyncratic, personal pathologies of a few writers, but it runs through the whole tradition. It shapes the conscious and unconscious symbolic universe of Jewish and Christian theology.

The second moment of feminist theology aims at the discovery of an alternative history and tradition that supports the full personhood of woman. This search takes many forms at the present time. It takes the form of biblical exegesis of Hebrew Scripture or New Testament to show that there are alternative traditions that affirm woman's full humanity, her equality in the image of God, her equal redeemability, her participation in prophecy, teaching, and ministry. It does not deny the reality of patriarchal bias, but it shows that, even amidst this bias, there are many fragmentary glimpses of alternative possibilities. Woman is there in the biblical drama, not just as object, but as subject. She acts as spokesperson of God and is affirmed as child of God and vehicle of redemptive Spirit.

Such a quest for alternative tradition also takes the form of new research into the histories of the church fathers, the Middle Ages, the Reformation, discovering and chronicling the church mothers who were there but whose story has been covered up and silenced. Such a quest in feminist theology does not confine itself to those who remained recognizably within "orthodox" traditions, the Paulas and Melanias of the fourth century, the medieval abbess, or the Reformation pastor's wife. It also moves into a larger sphere in traditions that have been buried, rejected, and declared heretical by the orthodox tradition: Montanists and Gnostics in the early church; Beguines, Joachites, and Waldenses in the Middle Ages; radical Baptists, Levelers and Diggers, Quakers and Shakers in the English Reformation; mystics, utopians, and transcendentalists in American Christianity.

In searching out these byways of the tradition, feminist theology discounts the judgment of orthodoxy against them which defines them as out of bounds for defining theological truth. It reads these traditions with an open mind, receptive to their insights and struggles for authenticity on their own terms. But feminist theology does not simply reverse orthodoxy, judging all that is traditionally orthodox as corrupt and all that has been marginalized as uncorrupted truth. Rather, it applies the same criteria of judgment to these marginal traditions and finds them partial at best. The very effort to assert an alternative in the face of the weight of dominant tradition, usually backed up with persecuting power, took its toll on these groups. They often could express their own alternative insights only in a fanatical form, typically expressed through anticreational dualisms.

The search for usable tradition may widen to pre-Christian, non-Christian, and post-Christian traditions, not simply over against the biblical and Christian traditions, but as a way of placing it in a larger context, which complements and corrects its biases. Inevitably, there is a hermeneutical circle in this quest. One has a working hypothesis of what a holistic perspective might mean, of woman within humanity, of humanity within creation, of creation grounded in God/ess. One seeks to find reflections of this holistic vision in both the mainstream and the buried parts of the tradition. In so doing, one is also forced to expand and revise one's hypotheses, as possibilities of full human being emerge in unexpected ways from the recovered community of experience. One does not find the whole that one seeks fully anywhere, either in orthodoxy or in heterodoxy, either in scholastics or in mystics. But one finds touchstones of authentic being in all of them in different ways. Out of this quest one begins to assemble an alternative vision that is yet to be articulated.

The third moment of feminist theology, then, consists of the tentative effort to state that alternative vision with a new fullness and consistency. One begins to work through the basic keys to theological reflection: authority, the nature and action of the divine, creation, anthropology, the why and how of evil, the meaning of redemption, the process of conversion and transformation, of redemptive community, and the possibilities of a new heaven and earth. Even this use of the traditional outline of Christian systematics is tentative. Perhaps this too is the product of an androcentric mentality. One cannot know what is down the road except by walking through it and then testing the new vistas that appear.

In reconstructing particular theological ideas, such as sin and grace, the feminist theologian now assumes an enlarged tradition, one that can draw, in both a critical and a constructive way, from Paul as well as from the Gospel of Mary; from Margaret Fell as well as from Richard Baxter; from Julian of Norwich as well as from Thomas Aquinas. The inherited bias of acceptable versus rejected traditions is reevaluated. These various traditions now stand, not against, but side by side within the enlarged community of foremothers and forefathers whom one claims as one's community of historical experience.

This enlarged community of life and thought is played against one's own best sensibilities and insights from one's own experience to seek the authentic shape of truth and untruth about human possibilities and human realities. An understanding of God/ess, humanity, male and female, the cosmos within which we stand, the history of evil, and the possibility of reclaimed goodness then emerges in new form, one that, for the first time, includes woman and woman's experience and that is tested by woman's humanity. The patterns of sexism are stripped off and discredited. A theology that can speak of these touchstones of theology in a way affirming of woman's full and equivalent humanity begins to be glimpsed.

A word might be said here about the claims of "universality" implied here. It is impossible to be objectively universal, that is, to include concretely all human groups, all historical traditions, all perspectives in one's theology. To claim to do so is simply to set up an abstract ideology in which a new, perhaps enlarged, particularity claims to be the universal, but actually excludes many people, many traditions, in a way that renders them invisible. It is better to acknowledge that all our syntheses are necessarily particular. They are working paradigms of inclusivity for those traditions, those groups, with whom we have concretely to do in a particular historical community. We can speak, then, of a subjective intention of inclusivity without pretending that this working paradigm is itself, objectively, normal. Thus the kind of inclusivity that we seek here is one that includes the full humanity of women, through a working synthesis of traditions within a particular historical community, Western and Christian. But an infinity of other such syntheses could be made by other persons standing within other historical contexts: Jews, within their various traditions; Africans or Asians who might want to engage in a new synthesis of Christian and non-Christian traditions, etc.

For what or whom does a (Christian) feminist theologian carry out this work of destruction and construction, denunciation and annunciation? Fundamentally, the feminist theologian, equally with the male theologian, claims to do this work of theologizing within and for the church, within and for the community of redemption. But this community of redemption itself has been redefined and enlarged. The community of tradition which it remembers now draws on new ancestors and ancestresses. The mission of this community must now not only include woman and woman's ministry equally, but it must make the redemption of humanity from sexism central to its understanding of its mission.

Such an understanding of the message of the good news and the mission of the church will place the feminist renewal community in tension with much of the self-understanding of existing historical churches of various traditions. As it becomes evident that feminist renewal of the gospel is not just minor tinkering with externals of dress and language and personnel, but a major recentering of the agenda of the church itself, hostility will grow. Those who seek to press on to a fuller faith and praxis of inclusive Christianity may find themselves vis-à-vis their parental churches as early Christianity did in relation to its parental community:

> They will put you out of the synagogues [churches]; indeed, the hour is coming when whoever kills you will think he is offering service to God. (John 16:2)

As the community of renewal of the gospel faces this inevitable negativity from those whose power and privileges are challenged at the deepest level, the maturity of its own spirituality becomes all the more urgent. It is necessary not only to urge the renewal community to "love one another" but also to love "one's enemies" as well, without in any way minimizing the fact that enmity is real and serious. One must be prepared to suffer, and to lose much, if one is serious about gaining a larger whole. The feminist theologian should stand, not as an isolated intellectual, but as an "organic intellectual" within this community of renewal. This means that the vocation of the theologian is not to "do her own thing" in an ivory tower, but rather to act as the enabler of the community within which she stands. She is teacher and enabler of those processes by which the community itself theologizes upon its own lived praxis of redemption.

It is the task of the feminist theologian to clarify the vision and to make clear the criteria for testing what is authentic and what is inauthentic. Those of the community of the good news against sexism need the courage of their convictions, the confidence that indeed they are in communion with God/ess and with the good nature of things when they struggle against patriarchy, despite all claims of authority against them. But at the same time she must enable this community to distinguish the authentic claims of this truth from their own fallibility, sinfulness, and weariness. The situation of em-battlement and marginalization is not good for one's mental health, so it becomes all the more urgent to have a spirituality that can test and correct the spirits, distinguishing one's commitment to Wisdom from one's own tendencies to fall into triumphalism and paranoia. The feminist theologian must take seriously the task of providing the theological base for a mature, self-critical spirituality, even if this self-critical side of her task will create tension and conflict within the renewal community itself.

If this renewal community claims to speak for the authentic gospel, then it must also see itself as existing, not just for itself, but for the renewal of the historical churches. Despite all marginalization from historical institutions, it must nevertheless reject the sectarian men-tality. It speaks both over against but also within and for the Chris-tian community, judging sexism as a sin incompatible with the gospel and calling the church to repentance. Authentic renewal is at once radical and catholic, radical in its profound critique of the systems of untruth and injustice, and yet catholic in claiming the center. That center is the true mandate for human personhood and society that can affirm our divinely intended selves, female and male. That true centering point is one that is not co-opted by the existing systems of evil, nor does it succumb to an alienation that can no longer affirm the humanity of the other. It is the task of theological reflection on one's praxis as church to constantly find that centering point amidst shifting historical realities.

How can feminist theology exercise such a praxis of renewal within the existing historical churches today? The institutional base for such a praxis of renewal is very difficult to find. On the one hand, local churches of established denominations either reject the legitimacy of such a critique or else allow it only in the most token and minimal way. Attendance at church becomes an increasingly frustrating experience for those who have glimpsed something of the radical character of this question. The situation is not much better in theological seminaries. A few seminaries allow the legitimacy of the question to the extent of allowing for an occasional generalist course on the subject taught by someone marginal to the faculty and without credibility in the general curriculum. A few others have moved to the point of allowing more specialized courses in particular fields, such as theology, Bible, church history, or pastoral psychology, but such courses are still thought of as "special interest" courses for women and a few "odd" men, and not as a challenge to the foundational curriculum which remains unchanged. The operating assumption of most seminaries is that androcentric theology is the "real" theology. Only here and there has it become possible even to raise the question of what it might mean to integrate the feminist issues into the foundational courses in such a way as fundamentally to transform what is regarded as normative tradition. Yet nothing less than this can satisfy the authentic feminist agenda.

It would appear, then, that feminist theology must pursue a double institutional strategy. This double strategy is not an "either-or," but a "both-and." Feminist theology must continue to argue its case with the mainstream institutions, within local churches, church conferences, and seminaries. It must build a base within these structures where it can dialogue with them. On the other hand, it also needs to establish autonomous bases not controlled by established church institutions, but in conversation with them. Examples of these are the Grailville Feminist Theology Quarter which was accredited through United Theological Seminary in Dayton, Ohio, but was run autonomously by a staff of women based at the Grail community. The Women's Theological Center in Boston, Massachusetts, similarly seeks to build an autonomous program with its

own funding and staff that could provide a year's accredited theological work in feminist theology and praxis for seminarians as well
as provide seminars and programs for women in the community. It
is accredited by the Episcopal Divinity School and Emmanuel College, but is in charge of its own agenda.

Another important example of autonomous feminist programs is
WATER (Women's Alliance for Theology, Ethics, and Ritual) in
Washington, D.C. This program seeks no official accreditation from
established institutions, but intends to create a network where women
can engage in action and worship, as well as theological reflection,
independently of church or seminary structures. A more short-term
example of this strategy is the Women's Summer Internship Program developed by the Feminist Theological Coalition in Chicago.

The Feminist Theological Coalition is an informal network of feminist scholars and ministers, mostly associated with the theological
seminaries of the Chicago area. It developed a summer internship
program for the summer of 1983 which placed women seminarians
in training with women pastors in inner-city churches. Theological
reflection and feminist social analysis were then carried out for a
six-week period based on this experience of ministry of women with
women in the city churches. The program was accredited by Garrett-
Evangelical Theological Seminary and Lutheran School of Theology,
but it obtained most of its own funding and planned its program
and chose its staff independently. Although it was only planned for
one summer, it was hoped that it could be a model that could be
imitated by networks of women in churches and seminaries in many
other cities. Interest in such a program for future summers has
already been expressed by a group in Toronto and another in Van-
couver. Funding was obtained through an implementation grant
from the American Theological Society and from Methodist, Episcopal, and Presbyterian women's groups.

The importance of such autonomous programs is that it is possible
in this context to explore the feminist questions of theology and
ministry thoroughly and radically instead of being constrained by
an unsympathetic or hostile context. Yet it is important that the two
strategies, the "inside" strategy within established church structures
and the "outside" strategy of autonomous groups not be seen as
mutually exclusive, but as complementary in a dynamic way. It is

not infrequently the case that women working as ministers or teachers in established church structures lend their help, usually with little remuneration, to autonomous networks as well. The theological work in the autonomous networks can then feed back into established structures, and the foothold in the established structures enables the autonomous networks to have some credibility and avenues of communication.

The feminist theologian, then, is called to do theology both within and for the church, and yet against its millennia-old heresy of sexism. To take this vocation seriously will necessarily transform and redefine all the traditional articles of theology. But it also means calling theology out of intellectual or academic abstraction into being a means by which the church itself reflects on its own praxis and its mission to the world.

3
Theology as Critical Reflection and Liberating Praxis

JOSÉ MÍGUEZ-BONINO

A "chicken and egg" question is hidden in this title: in order to define the task of the theologian one should know what is the nature and purpose of "theology." But, in another perspective, one should say that, historically, theology is what the "theologian" does. This is not merely a play on words; it points to a basic dialectic in our subject: the relationship of the historical to the theoretical, of the autonomy to the social relatedness of theology. And this, I submit, is a crucial question for theology today. In this presentation, I will attempt to raise this question in reference to our Latin American experience, not because I think that it is exemplary—a model to be copied or followed—but simply because it is the one I know and can analyze with some authenticity. Besides, since we all live in the same world (although not in the same part of the world or under the same conditions), this experience should not be totally irrelevant for you.

I have chosen a rather unsystematic pattern. My purpose is to offer some background and framework for raising questions around our theme rather than to set out a theory. I shall first try very briefly to characterize Latin American "liberation theology" as we see it, in order to raise afterward four questions: (1) the subject of theology—*who* does theology? (2) the location of the theologian—*from where* is theology done? (3) the relationship between praxis and theory—*how* do we do theology? and (4) theology and the socio-historical project—*what is the historical aim* of our theological work?

A Pastoral Theology

The theology of liberation understands itself as *a pastoral theology* in the sense of being a reflection on what the church—the Christian and the Christian communities—is doing and should do. In this sense it intends to be a critical service to mission. This is reflected in the fact that practically all theologians have direct responsibilities in church and community (sometimes theology is practiced almost as an avocation). All reflection has, to be sure, an element of speculation, but (as we shall have the opportunity to underline later) such speculation has its origin and goal in the questions raised by the life and witness of the church in the world.

At the same time, this theology finds its place in the history of theology in the range of what could be called the *theologies of salvation* as different from "theologies of revelation." That is, it is more interested in questions of life than in questions of meaning. Its main question is how can the Christian faith transform human life and situations rather than how can it give meaning to or clarify the meaning of life. Again, it hardly needs saying that transformation demands clarification, that revelation and redemption cannot be separated. But we are dealing here with an order of priority, not with a reduction of one discourse to another.

A third characteristic could be described by saying that the theology of liberation is a *historical theology,* both in the sense of being aware of its historical locus (and consequently also of the historical location of all other theologies) and of pursuing a reflection projected in historical (for instance, over against "metaphysical" and/or "subjective") categories. This attempt to overcome a purely metaphysical (for instance, the scholastic) and subjective (for instance, modern) frame of interpretation does not reject or eliminate those categories but privileges the categories of history. In this respect it is related to European "political" theologies and leans heavily on the Old Testament work of scholars like Gerhard von Rad who have shown the deeply historical character of the biblical witness.

Finally, it may not be redundant to say that the theologians who are engaged in this work intend to carry on a *theological* reflection, that is, a reflection which, even if it takes place in a context of commitment to the struggle of liberation and even if it makes ample use of sociological and political categories, nevertheless recognizes the integrity of theological thinking. It does not intend to substitute sociology for theology, but it respects the "epistemological break" introduced by the particular logos and structure of theology. Theology is related to the praxis, and more specifically in this case to the social praxis, of Christians, but it is not a mere reflection or mirroring of that praxis. The questions that emerge in Christian social praxis must be articulated and dealt with within the sphere of competence and with the instruments of theological thinking. It is in the context of these characteristics—a pastoral, soteriological, historical, theological reflection—that we approach now the four questions raised earlier.

The Subject of Theology

Who does theology? The answer seems obvious: "the church, the believing community." But in this connection, as in many others, the church is a complex and differentiated subject. It seems to me that the question can be somewhat clarified if we distinguish at least four instances within that subject in relation to the question, Who does theology? The first instance is *the gathered church*, the religious and cultic community which in its liturgy, its fellowship, its administration, and its service reflects and enacts a certain understanding of the gospel, sometimes verbalized or made explicit, more often only implied, but in any case powerfully operative. A second instance is *the institutionally appointed teaching church*, that is, the people officially charged with, and authorized for, the transmission of the Christian understanding, including the several levels from the catechist up (or down) to the professional theologian.[1] The third instance I shall call *the charismatic*, by which I mean people who feel attracted to theological (or philosophico-, or socio-, or cultural-theological) reflection and expression, whether officially recognized or not. We have here the artist, the prophet, the reformer, the philosopher. These may be either individuals or groups. Sometimes they live and work at the periphery of the visible church, or even totally outside it and in open revolt against the Christian faith and community. Nevertheless they offer powerful theological insights. The meaning of this assertion will be clear when we mention names such as Freud, Nietzsche, Daly, Bloch—to name only some of the modern examples. Finally, there are the *Christian people* (as a sociological reality), who live their faith (more or less consciously or faithfully) and who in their actions, their mores, their expressions, their struggles and sufferings reveal a certain under-standing and dynamic of the faith which (whether we regard it positively or negatively) determines the collective appropriation and operation of the faith much more strongly than the systematic teach-ing that the church intends to give. In the last analysis, the cultural transmission of that faith, the modification that it undergoes through different historical circumstances, its interaction with the official ministries of the churches, are normally the decisive factors in shap-ing the face of Christianity at a given time.

The purpose of this rather superficial analysis is simply to under-line the importance of the *relation* and *articulation* of these different instances. A simple diagram of the possible relations would pose some of the conditions in which theology has been and is now developed. In Latin America we are particularly concerned with the divorce between the first two instances (particularly the second, the teaching church) and the last. Charismatics—prophets and art-ists—have often been in closer relation to the people but very loosely related to the first two instances. The conditions in which the Christian faith was introduced in Latin America, as the religion of the conqueror, the identification of the institutional church, through its hierarchy, with the colonial power and its later siding with the conservative economic elites, its alliance with neocolonialism (in this case Protestantism shares the same characteristic), give to this cleavage a "class" character. While the teaching church has consis-tently been sociologically part of the dominant classes, the Christian "people" have been massively from the marginal and oppressed.[2] In Latin America, the emergence of "base communities"—no doubt the most fundamental development in Latin American Christianity in this century—provides a significant framework for a new theo-logical reflection insofar as it brings together, within the conditions of actual historical circumstances, these two instances (the teaching church and the Christian people), through a specific "option" or choice on the part of sectors of the teaching church (a subject to which we shall return). We realize, of course, that the particular form in which these different instances of the "theological subject" are related in Latin America differ from other contexts. But it seems to us that the basic question can and should be raised in any context.

The Location of the Theologian

Now I would like to speak of the theologian in a more restricted way, as the person who (whether professionally or not) makes of theological reflection his or her dominant praxis. Such a person, as anyone who pursues a particular discipline, has a double location in reality: on the one hand, within the area of his or her discipline with its particular epistemological conditions and demands, its corpus and methods, and, on the other hand, as a social agent in a particular place within a social formation. I think we can say that, while the theologian has been generally aware of the first location, we have only recently realized the significance of the second. Questions such as: Who is this theologian? What place has she or he in society? To which class does he or she belong and which class provides her or his support? What explicit or implicit commitments has he or she assumed?—these questions have seldom been raised in the histories of theology.

Precisely because we have now become acutely aware of this set of questions it is particularly important that we do not fall prey to a sociological determinism and come to regard the theological task as merely a reflection of a social location. There are at least three sets of considerations that should prevent us from doing this, and I will simply enumerate them here (although a fuller discussion would be necessary in any systematic treatment of the problem). The first is the need to recognize—even in a sociological analysis— the relative autonomy of the different instances of society, in this case the "religious" instance—an autonomy that must be recognized however one will want to answer the question as to whether any of these instances is "determinant" in the last analysis. The second consideration is the recognized fact that, if a particular "situation" within social reality (in a class or group, social formation, etc.) is a given, as human beings we can position ourselves in relation to that reality; in other words, a social option is a human possibility, however one will want to explain it sociologically or psychologically. Third—and most important in our context—theology has its own status. It cannot be a sanctified sociology but has to think through the impact of a social location and option in terms of the particularity of theological knowledge, a knowledge that has a form of apprehension, an epistemological principle—faith—and a fundamental reference—God (in the Christian faith, God's revelation in a special history, fulfilled in Jesus Christ).

If we take this double location seriously, the question that we have to ask ourselves in terms of the vocation of the theologian is how can the significance of the social location be evaluated, without avoiding the specificity of the theological task. There are at least three ways of looking at this question.

1. Social location (whether the simple result of "belonging" or of "option") determines a *perspective* on social reality. It has an enabling and a limiting effect; it makes possible to see certain things and it hides others. In Latin America we have sometimes spoken in this connection of "the epistemological privilege of the poor." We could as well point out that the bourgeois perspective of nineteenth-century (particularly Protestant) theology opened the eyes to certain areas of human reality—for instance, individual moral consciousness and subjectivity—and closed them to other areas— for instance, the eschatological element of the gospel. One could ask how can theologians of the first world see a reality which their social location forecloses? As a class problem, this is also the question for the Latin American theologian. The search for models through which this blinding effect of a social location can be overcome is one of the concrete issues that a theologian of liberation has to ask and solve, not merely in theoretical terms but in actual life.

2. Social location influences our *choice of relevant subject*. Work in any particular discipline imposes a choice, a decision about relevant, significant, fruitful questions and those which are considered to be secondary, misleading, or alienating. What, at a certain point in history, is worthy of being reflected upon (what Heidegger called *denkwürdig*)? The social perspective (as the relationship of personal commitment and social analysis) has a decisive influence in determining the relevance of particular topics or questions.

3. Finally, there is the question of the *destination* of our work: to which end is it related? There is, no doubt, a certain gratuity in any theoretical work worthy of the name; otherwise we fall into the

trap of opportunism and pragmatism. On the other hand, there is a priority of practice over theory. Theory is a necessary moment of reflection and has to be respected in its detachment. But such gratuity cannot hide the fact that all thinking has a social impact, that it has a performative significance (even if the thinker is not aware of it). We cannot today avoid the question, Whom are we serving? What is the social significance of what we do as theologians? At this point our social location and option have a decisive effect on our theologizing.

The Relation Between Praxis and Theory

The issues raised in relation to the previous questions point to one of the basic methodological questions for the theologian: the relation between praxis and theory. The theology of liberation has defined itself from the beginning as "a reflection on praxis." This has created a number of criticisms and misunderstandings.[3] Although we cannot now enter this discussion in depth, I would like to open it by introducing two observations made by Clodovis Boff in his very important book, *Teología do Político*.[4]

Boff suggests that reflection always turns around two foci which are in a certain tension. The relation between them can be understood undialectically by collapsing one of the foci into the other, or it can be understood dialectically. The following chart illustrates this point:

Pragmatism	PRAXIS	THEORY	Theoreticism
Determinism	WORLD	CONSCIOUSNESS	Utopianism
Positivism	FACTS	MEANING	Voluntarism
Empiricism	EXPERIENCE	TRUTH	Dogmatism
Realism	BEING	THOUGHT	Idealism

The pairs of concepts can easily be extended. The directions identified by the "isms" on both extreme columns mark the undialectical relations and therefore defective understanding of the relation. Over against it, Boff suggests (1) there is a methodological priority of praxis insofar as theory is a function of praxis and not vice versa (this does not mean a temporal priority as if pure praxis could exist but the fact that theory always takes place in the context of praxis and related to it) and (2) theory is the intervention of human thought (the possibility of taking distance, analyzing and abstracting) in praxis, that is, it introduces in praxis a specifically human factor making it into a "human praxis."

On the basis of this dialectical relation, Boff offers a diagram that illustrates false and authentic ways of relating theory and praxis in theology.

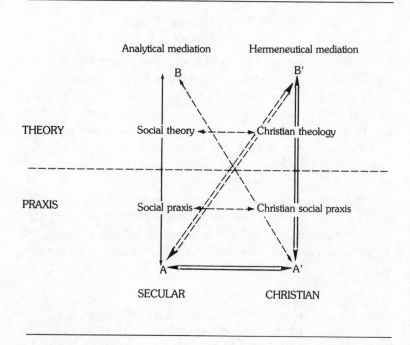

This diagram is not merely a theoretical construction. It presupposes certain theological and theoretical presuppositions, it embodies certain experiences, and it indicates certain directions for theological work:

1. It recognizes the distinction between praxis and theory. The latter rests on the former, but there is a dialectical relation in which neither of the two is merely passive or a simple reflection of the

other. This relation holds both for general and for specific (Christian) theory and praxis.

2. This horizontal division (the unity of all theory and all praxis) does not eliminate the vertical distinction of two sectors: the secular and the Christian. Such distinction will be questioned by many, but it seems to me correct and decisive both from a phenomenological and from a theologian point of view. It represents the specificity of faith which, however conceived, introduces a new "way of being and acting in the world." It does not deny our common humanity: "Christian social praxis" is human social praxis, and "Christian theology" belongs within human theoretical thinking (this is why A-A' and B-B' have been used as signs: each pair corresponds to the same reality, the ' sign marking a specificity within it).

3. The diagram can be useful for the study of several kinds of relations. We are now concerned with B', theological reflection, insofar as we are dealing with the specific vocation of the theologian. In this respect, the diagram points out some authentic and some misleading relations:

a. Christian theology incorporates the experience of social praxis through the praxis of Christians: as theology, it is not a reflection on social praxis in general but of social praxis as experienced and acted out by Christians. We in Latin America are becoming more and more convinced of the soundness of this view both from a positive and from a negative experience. On the one hand, it is only as a growing number of Christians have become committed to an active social praxis of liberation that a theological reflection has become both necessary and possible; more and more, the "base communities" and the other committed groups of Christians who reflect on their common social praxis as Christians have become a focus for theological reflection, a fruitful place for a new understanding of such issues as the relation of transcendence and incarnation, ecclesiology, the meaning of grace, etc. Negatively, we have also had the experience of theology built without this reference, on the basis of social analysis alone, and it tends to become a form of sociology of religion or an ideological discourse, quite useful and necessary in its own place but one that does not and cannot qualify as "theology." The need of this relation (represented in the diagram by the double full lines) and this excluded relation (represented by

the double broken line) becomes for the theologian a question of
life and not only of thought. Where are these reference groups of
Christian social praxis present? How is the theologian related to
them?

b. Christian theology incorporates the experience of social praxis
through general social theory: as theology it does not have a specifically Christian social theory; it has no particular access to social
reality. On the other hand, theology cannot avoid the mediation of
general human theoretical thinking: it has no "heavenly language"
to articulate its understanding. In relation to a theology articulating
critically Christian social praxis, it has to use the mediation of social
sciences, and, in this mediation, it incorporates an analysis and
understanding of secular social praxis and its commitments. This
has posed for the theologian (in our experience at least) some difficult
tasks, on the one hand, because social sciences have not been a part
of the traditional baggage of the theologian (usually loaded with
philosophy and lately some psychology). On the other hand, because, since no social (or any other?) science is purely objective or
neutral, it has meant making choices and commitments in relation
to social sciences which sometimes have been wrongly interpreted
as substituting ideology for faith (a danger always present but certainly no more than in the privileging of one or other philosophical
mediation, as theology has done for almost two millennia).

c. Incidentally, we can briefly comment on two other possible
relations. (1) Social theorists have every right to analyze Christian
social praxis; in fact, many of them in Latin America have lately
become interested in it and have variously interpreted such praxis
in sociological terms. This work is of great significance and the
theologian must take it seriously. But it should not be understood
strictly as "theology"; it cannot dispense the theologian (who, in
fact, sometimes may be the same person) from seeking the "hermeneutical mediation" which alone qualifies reflection as theological. (2) Christians also have a right (and a need) to resort to social
theory in relation to their social praxis. They cannot expect theology
to offer them the tools needed for this purpose. But, as Christians,
they cannot dispense with "theological interpretation" which means
not only the appropriation of some already elaborated theological
insights but the participation in a group of reference (or base com-

munity) where social praxis is reflected in the light of the Christian faith. Again, we have here, together with the very positive experience mentioned above, the painful one of Christians for whom their faith has lost all significance for their social praxis, leading either into a total loss of their (explicit) faith or to a schizophrenic existence in which social praxis and Christian faith do not nourish, correct, or support each other. The theological question flows again into an ecclesiological and pastoral one.

Theology and Sociohistorical Project

What we have said about the social location of the theologian and Christian social praxis finds a concrete focus in the question of a "social project." There are, in fact, no general, undefined social praxis and location: they are always specific and particular, situated in time and space. This raises the question of "a historical project," by which we mean the choice of a goal and a process for a society which is more concrete and specific than a mere utopia but more flexible and open-ended than a program. (As an illustration we can say that England in the eighteenth and nineteenth centuries or the United States in the Manifest Destiny era—or at least their dominant elites—have had a project and were able to mobilize the resources and forces of their societies in the pursuit of it). Such projects must be able to command vision and commitment, to awaken hope, and to elicit effort and sacrifice.

The Christian faith cannot help being related to such projects—supportively or critically, consciously or unconsciously.[5] In Western history, from the fourth century on (at least!), there has always been an important "religious" justification (and sometimes an important religious contestation) of the different projects in which nations, groups, or other social formations have engaged. The main projects that vie today in Latin America for the commitment of our people—what could be called the traditional-aristocratic, the liberal-modernizing, and the liberation project—represent not only clearly identifiable social sectors and interests, different social analysis and ideologies, but also conflicting interpretations of the Christian faith. I think similar (or analogous) analysis could be made of other societies. Are Christians aware of this relation? How is Christian theology related to these projects? What is the responsibility of the theologian in this respect? How can the theologian make options and choices? A number of issues arise in this respect: What is the role of "spiritual discernment" as a synthetic prophetic act in this choice? How is the collective consciousness of the churches related to individual or prophetic groups? And what is the amount of "social determination"—as class, for instance—that plays on this consciousness? How can we articulate a Christian ethical mediation in this choice and how is it related to social analysis? Such questions (basically the area of Christian political ethics) cannot be pursued here. But they point out the fact that "the vocation of the theologian" cannot be exercised in a vacuum, from a neutral and uncommitted place, but demands a specific historical commitment, with all the risks that this means but also with the possibilities that it offers.

NOTES

1. In a European context one would have to raise here the complex but crucial problem of the place of "the theological academic community." It seems to me that its double relation to the community of faith and to the academic community has never been consistently clarified and introduces an ambiguity in all its work.

2. Sometimes this situation has been described by using Gramsci's distinction between the "traditional" intellectual (related to the dominant class and therefore operating in the sense of the preservation of the existing society) and the "organic" intellectual, related to the class bearer of future history and therefore thinking in terms of transformation. A study of the traditional Latin American church teaching from this point of view could be both relevant and enlightening.

3. See, for instance, the criticisms of K. Lehmann in the framework of the International Theological Commission of the Vatican, "Problemas metodologicos y hermeneuticos de la 'teología de la liberación,' " in Teología de la liberación (Madrid: B.A.C., 1978), and of Methold Ferre, "En torno a la praxis," Víspera 29 (1972).

4. Clodovis Boff, Teología do Político e suas mediacoes (Rio de Janeiro: Vozes, 1978). This book constitutes, in my view, the most important presentation of the methodological presuppositions of the theology of liberation.

5. There are, of course, those who would claim that Christianity has a social-historical project of its own. Our comments on the realms of theory and praxis should make clear that we reject this possibility both for theological and for practical reasons.

4
Theology as a Public Vocation

GORDON D. KAUFMAN

In his novel of some years ago entitled *By Love Possessed*, James Cozzens makes a character, Julius Penrose, say, "If hypocrisy can be said to be the homage which vice pays to virtue, theology could be said to be a homage nonsense tries to pay to sense."

The English philosopher and theologian, I. M. Crombie, has said, "Theology is not a science; it is a sort of art of enlightened ignorance."

The logical positivist philosopher, A. J. Ayer, maintains that theology deals for the most part in meaningless assertions.

What is one to make of such negative, even cynical, assessments of theology? These may be particularly distressing when one remembers the medieval affirmation of theology as "the queen of the sciences," that science in which the very knowledge of God is to be had. Do these contemporary opinions mean that theology properly belongs to another age, that it has no real place in the modern intellectual world, and that it is essentially an outmoded form of superstition? Certainly Ayer, along with many others, would happily defend that sort of judgment. That theology is no longer a viable intellectual activity is a claim which must be given serious consideration. If this claim is true, then the vocation of theology must be thought of as having become fundamentally nonintellectual—or else as dying; and a calling to do theology as an intellectual activity cannot much longer have a place in the modern world.

Doubtless, theology could continue to serve the church, the company of religious believers who still think in terms of dedicating their lives to a supernatural being—God; and as long as such persons are around—and there is no reason to think they will not be around

for a good while—there would be a need for theologians to attempt
to explain and to interpret religious beliefs. Thus, there would still
be theological vocations, but they would be defined largely in parochial and institutional terms, as service to church and synagogue.
The theologian would have become basically an institutional func-
tionary, that is, one who understands himself or herself largely in
terms of the needs of the religious institution, one who performs
certain important functions for church or synagogue, namely, reflecting on and interpreting the beliefs of the religious group to itself
and to others who might be interested. Theology has often been
understood in this way, and this kind of theology is undoubtedly
useful and important. It is work that churches and other religious
groups need to have performed if they are to carry on their activities—just as they need responsible treasurers to keep their books,
and effective bureaucrats to manage their regional and national of-
fices, and custodians to care for their buildings and other properties.
But this is a conception in which the high calling suggested by the
very name "theology"—speaking or thinking about God, about the
ultimate reality with which we have to do, about that than which
nothing greater can be conceived—seems to have been almost completely lost.

To conceive of theology essentially in terms of the church's re-
quirements and needs amounts to a kind of ecclesiastical positivism,
for the tasks of theology are here understood as grounded simply
on the *givenness* of the church as an institution, on the happenstance
fact that churches exist in our society. Some, of course, will hasten
to reject this implication by reminding us that the church understands itself to be in a special way the arena of God's activity in the
world: theology, then, as a churchly activity, is grounded in and a
direct expression of God's own work. What broader or more significant basis for theology's high calling could be offered than that?
But to make this move involves a vicious circle, for on this view
theology is explained and grounded by ecclesiology, that is, by a
theological understanding of the church; but obviously, to develop
such a theological understanding of the church we must already
know what theology is and how it is to be done. Clearly, trying to
explain what theology is in terms of what the church is is to put the
cart before the horse. It is theology which interprets and explains

the church through developing an ecclesiology; it is not the church which explains and interprets theology. Except, then, in the strictly sociological sense that church traditions and church institutions have supported theological activity in the past, and continue to do so today, it is evident that the church does not provide theology with its real foundations, nor can the church define for us what theology is or should be as a vocation. An ecclesiastical interpretation of theology does not probe deeply enough to discover its real roots, and thus it does not enable us to discern the basic human significance of theological work.

There are four resources to which we can turn for light on our question. These are history, the study of religion, the study of philosophy, and then, finally, theology itself. Let us consider these in turn.

From one point of view, the question of what theology is and the question of what kind of vocation theology can be can best be answered historically. "Theology," after all, is first and primarily a word in the English language, and it can be understood only in that historical context; and the vocation of theology is clearly an activity or calling developed in Western culture, in the context of Western religious and educational institutions and intellectual disciplines. The subject matters with which theology deals, the problems it faces, the methods it has devised—all of these emerged in Western history. We can understand what this word means, then, and we can grasp what sort of vocation this is, what sort of intellectual discipline is involved here, only historically, only through seeing what each of these *has been* in the past. For none of these have any other being or meaning than their *historical* being and meaning. To answer our question about theology as a vocation, we will need to engage in careful and thorough historical studies of theological language, theological ideas, theological problems and methods, and these studies will enable us to see what theology is. Theology is essentially a *historical reality*.

All of this, it seems to me, is eminently true. Theology has grown up in a history and it has its very being and life in history. Historical study is certainly the proper place to begin any search for an understanding of the nature of theology and the calling of the theologian. Without historical understanding of what theology is, in the sense of what it has been, we will have no understanding at all of what theology is, in the sense of what it can be. For theology is an activity that has been created in and through a particular history, and it has no being apart from that history.

Yet a strictly historical investigation of theology would not be sufficient for our purposes. It could only tell us what theology *has been*, how it *has developed*; it could not tell us either what theology *is now*, or what it might be, or should become, in the future. And surely these questions are just as important for ascertaining the nature and possibilities of theology as is the historical question. Indeed, when we are asking about theology as a calling, as a vocation one might choose to enter, they are more important. Obviously, what theology is now and shall become is heavily dependent on its history, but it is not completely determined by that history. Though our search for an understanding of theology must be grounded in historical knowledge, it must extend beyond that. How can we move to such a wider vantage point?

The newly emerging discipline of religion studies may suggest itself as helpful here. Theology, as we have known it historically, has been a Western mode of religious reflection; perhaps if we break out of the parochialness of our Western religious traditions to an understanding of human religiousness in general—and an understanding of the place that reflection has had in other religious traditions—we will be in a position to understand not only what theology has been but what it might now become. There is much to commend this approach to our question. As we shall see in a few moments, the role in human life played by religious symbolism, and by critical reflection on and development of that symbolism, throws important light on the basic human significance of theological reflection and thus on the role that theology can play in human affairs.

But religion studies, like historical studies, are fundamentally descriptive in character. They can tell us much about the functions that intellectual reflection has fulfilled in the several religious traditions, and thus they can bring to light uses and meanings of theology which we might otherwise overlook, but they have no way of moving beyond this descriptive work to the development of criteria and standards for refining and reforming theology. Religion studies, no more than history, can present us with a new vision—or even just a proposal—of what theology might be, or should become, in the future. To the extent they attempt to do so, to the extent they attempt to define what "thinking about God" is really all about, what theology really comes down to, they must devote themselves to a critical and systematic assessment of the meaning of the symbol "God"—and not reduce its meaning to that prescribed by some general theory of symbolism—and that would be directly to engage in theological analysis and reflection. As we shall see in a moment, the symbol "God" makes such universal and comprehensive—indeed, imperial!—claims for itself as to defy reduction to or subsumption under any alien or independent analytical scheme or intellectual categories.

We can see this best and most directly, perhaps, by considering whether that most comprehensive of all human intellectual disciplines, philosophy, is not in a position to define the proper place and role of theology. It does not matter whether we understand philosophy in the classical sense of metaphysics, as dealing with the question of reality as such; or in the more modern sense, as a second-order critical discipline reflecting on the claims to knowledge of the other sciences, defining their proper arenas, their methods and their limits, and clarifying their interrelations with each other; or whether we think of it in that very contemporary way, as critically examining the various "language games" in which human beings are engaged, ascertaining the rules of each game and determining how each is properly played. In all these cases, philosophy seems to be giving a kind of overview or perspective—whether on reality as a whole or on human life and some of its activities—which should enable us to assign theology its proper place and role. And with that in mind, we should then be able to say something about the sort of vocation that theology is.

I do not want in any way to derogate the importance of such philosophical inquiries and of such a philosophical overview. Certainly, to the extent that theology wants to claim that God is *real*, it must take seriously the metaphysical inquiries of the philosopher into the question of what it is to be, what sort of structure the real has. And to the extent that the theologian claims to *know* anything at all, above all to know something of God, he or she must attend carefully to the epistemologists' studies about what can properly count as knowledge, how knowledge is gained, what its possibilities are and what its limits, how it can be distinguished from mere subjective opinion or belief. And inasmuch as theology is, after all, *talk*—talk about God—theology does well to listen carefully to what the linguistic philosophers have to say about the possibilities and the limits of human talk in general, and especially about the "deep grammar" of our language about God. There is a great deal to be learned from philosophy about the nature of theology, and thus about the proper tasks of theology and the methods that theologians can employ. In short, philosophy can teach us much about the sort of vocation that theology can be and how that vocation can best be carried out.

But a finally authoritative answer to our question cannot be found here either. However much philosophy might have a certain legitimate superintendency over the other human disciplines and activities, we dare not grant it ultimate authority over theology. At most, we can allow that theology and philosophy stand in a kind of dialectical relation to each other. Though the philosopher asks questions about the nature of reality as such and seeks to ascertain the possibilities and the limits of all human knowledge, indeed of all language, the theologian, as the word itself suggests, and as our historical researches confirm, is involved in "thinking about God," in "speaking of God," that is, the theologian is involved in inquiry into that ultimate point of reference in terms of which all else—all reality, all knowing, all speaking, all experiencing, indeed all philosophy!—is to be understood. In attempting to speak of God, the theologian is attempting to articulate that in terms of which everything else without exception must be grasped, if it is to be understood correctly, if it is to be understood truly.

In our tradition, "God" has been conceived as "the creator of the heavens and the earth," as "the lord of history," as "the ground of being," as "the source of all that is," as "the absolute, unconditional reality," "that than which nothing greater can be conceived," "the alpha and the omega." These are very diverse modes of expression with quite distinct meanings, but in one respect they are simply different ways of making essentially the same point: that by "God" we mean that behind or beyond which we cannot go in any experience, any thought, any act of imagination; we mean that which circumscribes and limits all else, that which relativizes every other reality—including especially, of course, ourselves and our thinking—that which is, therefore, the ultimate point of reference in terms of which everything must be understood if it is to be understood rightly. If, then, theology—disciplined "thinking about God"—is to be true to itself and its subject matter, it will have to be in terms of that very subject matter—God—that theology finally comes to understand itself; not in terms of some other reality, or in the terms some other discipline, such as philosophy or history or religion studies, might assign to it. Theology's responsibility is finally only to *God*. And since what we mean by God, what we can say about God, is the special task of theology itself to determine, since the significance of our talk about God, and the possibilities and the limits of that talk, are issues to which theology must quite properly address itself, it appears that theology itself must finally decide what theology is or can be.

Theology (like philosophy) is a *reflexive* activity. Unlike disciplines such as chemistry or biology or music, which study objects other than themselves, theology and philosophy in studying their objects must develop theories of themselves as well as of their objects—because they are themselves included within the objects they are trying to understand. Any philosophical theory of reality or of knowledge which does not or cannot explain what sort of reality philosophy itself is, and what sort of knowledge it attains, is obviously deficient. Every philosophy must include a theory of itself; philosophy is a reflexive discipline. Similarly theology: any interpretation of that ultimate point of reference in terms of which all else must be understood, which does not include an explanation or interpretation of theology itself in terms of that point of reference, is clearly deficient. Theology is also a reflexive discipline and must include a theory of itself in connection with its theory of God. And, by the same token, philosophy and theology will each include theories of the other; they are dialectically related to each other. Each can throw light on the other, but neither dares abdicate its responsibility of self-direction and self-definition to the other; each must ultimately understand itself as autonomous and free in relation to all other disciplines.

To what point has our investigation brought us? We are seeking to understand what theology might be as a vocation. We have inquired into a number of ways of getting at that question, including historical study, the study of religion, and philosophical reflection. As we have reflected on what these disciplines can teach us of theology, however, we have been led to conclude that it is theology itself which ultimately must define what theology is, for only in the light of theology's own most fundamental subject matter, God, can it be rightly understood.

Now, perhaps, we are in a better position to understand some of the witty and cynical gibes at theology which we noted at the beginning. What kind of nonsense is it to say that theology must and can define itself, especially if it must do so with reference to God? For who, after all, is to say what or who God is? And how would such a one know? What do any of us know about "the ultimate point of reference" in terms of which everything is to be understood? Is it not the emptiest sort of speculation to pretend to know something about that from whence all this vast universe has come, and why it is here—that is, to claim to know the creator of the heavens and the earth? Doubtless there are ancient myths both in and out of the Bible which speak of such matters, but what intellectually sophisticated and critical person today would even venture so much as an opinion on such things? If theology must understand itself in terms of such a vast unknowableness as this, then surely it is *nonsense*; and to the extent to which it tries to explain itself, tries to give reasons for its own being and its own activities, for the sort of nonsense that it is, it is a kind of homage that nonsense attempts to pay to sense. But it is a very nonsensical homage indeed. Theology appears to be the attempt to deal with that which is in principle inaccessible to us, in principle unknowable. Philosophy at least, even in its most pretentious forms, attempts only to deal with the Real, so far as we can know it. But theology is the attempt to speak of, rationally to grasp, a transcendent or ultimate point of reference. That is too much. Surely human beings should confine themselves to more modest vocations.

I shall not take the way out of this dilemma suggested by Karl Barth and others of the last generation. For such persons, though it was readily admitted that we by our own powers could not know God, it was maintained that God can, if God so chooses, reveal

Godself to us, grant us knowledge as a gratuitous gift which we can only acknowledge thankfully. As Barth frequently said, with one side of his mouth, there is no solution at all to this problem of the knowledge of God, if what we are asking for is an explanation of how we, finite sinful human beings that we are, have the power to know God: we have no such powers at all—just the point I have been making here. With the other side of his mouth, however, Barth found himself able to speak thousands and thousands of words about this God of whom we human beings have the power to know precisely nothing. There seems to be some sort of problem here— a problem, however, with which we shall not tarry now.

I want to return to my text about the homage which nonsense must pay to sense. However difficult, however impossible is the theological task, it is one that cannot be avoided. We are beings who must seek to understand and to know, and this not just because of the pleasure or the joy we are given through knowing. If that were the case, to be "lovers of wisdom"—philosophers—would be an optional activity, a pastime for the wealthy and the leisured, as philosophy indeed has often been.

No, we must seek to know and to understand for much deeper reasons than that. It is because we are beings who must *act*, because we are agents, who make decisions and take actions that affect our- selves and others this day, this week, the next few years, possibly a lifetime or more. There is no way we can avoid deciding, avoid acting, avoid taking responsibility. This is a very heavy burden upon us; as Jean-Paul Sartre said, we are "condemned to be free." But we are able to decide and to act only if we know something about the situation in which we are living, the situation which called forth this act from us, and only if we know something about our own powers and potentialities, about what we are able to do in this situation. Moreover, we are able to make decisions only if we have the capacity to imagine different possible acts which we might per- form and can envisage the consequences of each such act with some reliability; and only if we have criteria enabling us to assess the several possibilities available to us so we can choose which to ac- tualize. In short, only if we have a good bit of knowledge of the world and of the possibilities open to us in the world, and knowledge about ourselves and our possibilities, as well as knowledge of those others round about us with whom we are interacting, will it be possible for us to decide and act at all. Knowledge, then, is no dispensable luxury for any of us, even if we are the humblest workman or the most illiterate peasant. Some sense of the world, and of the human place and human possibilities within the world, and of our position in all of this, is needed by each of us.

For the most part, it has been in and through the human imagination's creation of religious myths and traditions that pictures of the world, and stories of the human place and task within that world, have been developed, gradually becoming promulgated throughout whole societies over many generations. These pictures and stories have been many and various in human history, and we cannot begin to examine them here. I want to point out, however, how absolutely indispensable such pictures and stories are to human beings, with their need for orientation in life. Without them, human action, and the taking of responsibility for action, would be impossible. Please note: I am not saying these pictures or stories are *true*, that human beings in their various religious traditions have come to know the *truth* about the world and about themselves; I am saying, rather, that they are indispensable. Without them, human beings would simply be unable to act and thus unable to take responsibility for themselves and their lives. We must have a world view, a conceptual scheme, within which to order all of the "blooming, buzzing confusion" of life, as William James called it, or else we could not live and act at all; our great religious traditions have provided us with such world pictures.

With this perspective which the historical and the sociological study of religion brings us, we can see more clearly the role and task, and the human significance, of theology, with its concern for "the ultimate point of reference" in terms of which all else is to be understood. Theologians have been attempting to grasp and to understand and to set forth a picture of the world and of human life which has "God" as its focal center, and which seeks, thus, to see and understand all else in relation to God and God's activity. The vocation of theology, like reflection in other religious traditions, seeks to serve the human need to find orientation in the world and in life—not immediate or proximate orientation for this present moment of experience or this particular small decision; such orientation might be provided by pop psychology or simply by the regularities of custom or habit. Rather, theology is concerned with that underlying human task of finding orientation for the long haul, for life as a whole, orientation for one's children and one's children's children, for one's whole society, indeed for all of humanity. How is orientation of that order and that magnitude to be found? How can it be assessed and by what criteria criticized? How can it be transformed for greater adequacy? These are the questions to which the great religious traditions address themselves, and these are the issues which the intellectual reflection and the search for understanding within those traditions have pursued. In the West it has been preeminently theology which has concerned itself with this set of issues, and it is to this set of issues that one must be prepared to give oneself if one takes up theology as a vocation.

The question about human orientation in life is framed largely, for those of us in the Judeo-Christian tradition, in terms of what H. Richard Niebuhr has called "radical monotheism." For this perspective meaning and value and being are not diffused into several different foci, into a variety of gods or powers; rather, they are all focused in one central point—*God*—which is taken as "the ultimate point of reference" for understanding everything, every value, every experience, every desire, every act of imagination. In this world view, thus, everything is brought together into a single ultimate order, instead of always being under the threat of disintegration into unrelated multiplicities and finally into chaos. By "God" we mean that—whatever it is—which holds together all of this multiplicity and richness of experience in a significant unity, that from which it all ultimately comes and to which it all must go. But God has been more than simply the alpha and the omega of life. In the Judeo-Christian tradition, God is seen as a fundamentally moral reality, one characterized by justice and goodness, mercy and truth, as well as by the power to create and to destroy. So human moral existence also, and the human pursuit of value and truth and meaning, must be understood as grounded in God and oriented properly only when in relation to God. Our Western monotheistic heritage enables us to raise questions about the ultimate unified grounding of all dimensions of existence and all features of the world, and thus to see all of life "steadily and whole," to use again the words of William James. It is the special vocation of theology, working with its great symbol "God"—made available to us by our tradition—to attempt to specify what this can mean for our times, our lives, our problems. That is, it is the special vocation of theology to consider how "God" is to be understood today, and how we are to be understood as "under God."

If theology is centrally concerned with the question of God, as I am contending here, and if that concern means that the theologian's responsibility must ultimately be to God, then the major error or aberration or confusion into which a theologian may fall is idolatry, giving principal attention to objectives and goals and values other than or less than God. There are several idolatries that are especially tempting for theologians. The service of the church, for example— the work of the church, the needs of the church as an institution, these are undoubtedly of great importance to theology. But they must never become theology's driving motivation; that would be to put an idol in the place where only God can rightly be. Again, the interests of the university in the impartial pursuit of truth, the need of the humanities for an adequate understanding of human religiousness, and thus the importance of helping the study of religion to become a well-recognized academic discipline, the desirability of entering into dialogue with literature and the arts, with history and philosophy and the sciences—all of these objectives are worthy and important to contemporary theology. But these interests and demands arising in the university setting of much theological work must never be allowed to divert the theologian from his or her central responsibility: that of dealing seriously and critically with the question of God. The principal standard of judgment with which theological work should be pursued is not the question of truth and falsity, or good and evil, or right and wrong, or beauty and ugliness, however important each of these contrasts may be; the principal theological standard should be the one implicit in the conceptual distinction of God and the idols, a standard that takes up into itself all these others and gives them their proper place and significance.

Because the theologian's central criterion of judgment is "the ultimate point of reference" in terms of which all else must be understood, theology is—at least potentially—critical theory par excellence. Theology must not allow itself to be diverted from that fundamental task and responsibility. Failing to be fully critical, including especially failing to be fully self-critical—that is, critical of all its own concepts and symbols, its own procedures, its own objectives, its own traditions, critical of the institutions and the social structures that support it—would be to fail to be theology. To be one, then, who reflects critically on God and the idols, and one who understands how that reflection applies not only to our world and our society but also to himself or herself and all with which he or she is involved, is to be a theologian. To take this up as one's lifework is to accept theology as one's vocation.

Having spoken of the central concern and responsibility of theology, we are now in a position to say something about the web of relations within which theological work is carried on. The question of God—of "the ultimate point of reference"—cannot be dealt with completely in the abstract. One always begins one's reflection on such matters with a concrete and particular conception of God, a conception mediated by a particular tradition of religious life and reflection. It is because the conception presented by tradition has been found meaningful and nourishing that the concept of God first grasps one as worthy of attention and respect and even of the devotion of a lifetime. It is out of and on the basis of one's Baptist or Presbyterian past, one's Christian or Jewish experience, or at least on the basis of Western religious reflection and literature, that one comes to think about the question of God at all and is impressed with its import and urgency. And so we are, first of all, Christian theologians or Jewish theologians, sectarian Protestant or Roman Catholic theologians, attempting to understand who or what God is in the light of those traditions which have formed us.

There is, however, a dialectical tension between the tradition that has formed us and given us our conception of God and the *ultimacy* of this point of reference, of which we have become aware through the tradition. As theologians we necessarily dig ever deeper into our tradition that we might better grasp the God that is mediated through it; but at the same time, as theologians, we become ever more sensitive to the faults and failures in our tradition in the light of the claims of that God to which it has been so inadequately responsive. The theologian must necessarily and continuously drink deeply from the Bible and the best of biblical scholarship, and from the many great reflective writers of past and present, even while learning to take up a critical stance over against all of these in the name of that very God of whom they also spoke. An outstanding example in recent years of the way in which the tradition continues to nourish the very criticism of itself and its own most basic and sacred documents is to be found in our growing consciousness that the almost exclusive use of the masculine gender in our language and images of God is theologically intolerable. That such radical criticism of the tradition, reaching back all the way to its biblical roots, can appear and be taken seriously, is one of the most encouraging signs of the continuing vitality of theological reflection in our time.

Theologians, then, are heavily dependent on scholarship in the historical and biblical fields, and must regularly attend to the work being done in those areas; without such continuous nourishment in tradition, theological activity could not proceed. But theology is equally dependent on work in the natural and the social sciences, in secular history and in philosophy. For it is the God of all the universe—"the creator of the heavens and the earth"—which theology is seeking to understand and to interpret, and this cannot be done without some grasp of the way in which the world and humankind are interpreted in the best knowledge available to us today. If one is to take up theology as a vocation, one must have an interest in the whole wide range of human experience and knowledge, and one must be prepared to bring this into relationship with that ultimate point of reference we call God. In our time, the poets and the philosophers and the psychologists have taught us much about the self-deception and the ideological self-justification to which the human spirit so often falls prey in all its intellectual activities; these insights, also, must be incorporated into the self-critical self-consciousness of the theologian alert to the dangers of idolatry. In the vocation of theology there must be an openness to new insight and new understanding from any and every perspective or point of view; there is no room for parochial preference for one's own tradition or community or one's own familiar values and ways of thinking. Contemporary theological work is dependent upon, and must be prepared to relate itself to, the wide diversity of human experiences and modes of consciousness and the whole range of human cultures. But all this must be approached, examined, and assessed critically, with an eye to that ultimate point of reference, God, in terms of which each nuance and each idiosyncracy finds its proper place.

By now it will be clear to all of you, I am sure, that theology as I envisage it is an impossible task. That is true. How, after all, can we talk of God? How is it possible for us to think of God? Surely, as Crombie has said, theology cannot be a science; we—all of us—are simply much too ignorant to pretend that we can really know what we are doing when we are seeking to do theology. No one can claim to be, in the proper sense of the word, a "theologian." Yet, as we have seen, however difficult it may be, orientation in human affairs is absolutely indispensable for human life; the attempt to do as much as we can toward ordering life in relationship to that ultimate point of reference in terms of which every reality finds its proper place—in which we are centered on God and not on some deceiving idol—simply dare not be given up, however difficult or impossible it might seem. The repeated and persistent shipwrecks to which our all-too-human idolatries inevitably bring us make careful theological reflection and study imperative. Our idolatrous anthropocentrism has brought us to near-destruction of the ecological web which sustains life on this planet. Our idolatrous ethnocentrisms and egocentrisms have brought us to near-destruction of all human life and human culture. Concern for the earth, then, and concern for our fellow human beings everywhere require us to attend to the problem of our fatal idolatries; they lay upon us an imperative to do theology with diligence and with care.

I have said that the ultimate responsibility of the theologian is to God, and that secondarily, therefore, the theologian has a responsibility to the traditions out of which our "God-talk" emerged and which have nourished that talk, as well as to the other academic and cultural traditions of humankind. But now we can see that theologians also have a responsibility to the earth and to all of humankind living on this earth. To take up the vocation of theology is to commit oneself to assuming these responsibilities to God, to the order of nature within which we live, and to our fellow human beings, as one's lifework.

Very little has been said here about specifically Christian theol-

ogy. I hope it will be clear, from what I have said of the importance
of tradition, that this is not because I do not value such theology
highly; as you all know, I think of myself as primarily a Christian
theologian. So far as Christ enables us better to understand who
God is, and thus better to grasp that ultimate point of reference in
terms of which all else must be understood, we must attend to the
nature and work and significance of Christ, we must do Christian
theology. It is important, however, that Christ not displace God in
the order of our thinking and valuing. There can be Christ idolatries,
Christolatries and Jesusolatries, as well as other sorts. The Christian
church, I am sorry to say, has often been guilty of such Christ
idolatry, particularly, perhaps, in its metaphysical interpretations of
the person of Christ and in its claim that outside the sphere of Christ
there is no salvation. Jews and Muslims have long insisted that this
was a Christian perversion, and both Muslims and Jews—particularly Jews in this century—have suffered much at the hands of
Christians and others, partly because of the fanatical and idolatrous
uses to which Christian symbolism has all too easily lent itself. In
our day, conscious as we are of the horrors of the Holocaust, we
must be especially careful not to make the mistake of thinking of
theology as simply or primarily *Christian* theology. Theology is first
and foremost "thinking about God," not "thinking about Christ."
Our thinking about Christ, also, must subserve our thinking about
God, lest it become one more perverse and idolatrous human intellectual activity.

At the beginning of this essay I suggested that we must take very
seriously the assertion of some that theology is an outmoded form
of intellectual activity, and therefore it must be considered a dying
vocation. Having now made some proposals about the way in which
theology should be understood, let me return to that claim. I hope
that it is obvious that the question of misplaced commitments and
loyalties in human affairs—what I have discussed in terms of the
theological rubric of idolatry—is no passing or temporary phenomenon; it is a continually recurring problem in human life everywhere.
The issue, then, of God and the idols—of those affections and commitments which are fulfilling and redemptive, and those which are
corrupting, diseased, and destructive—is still with us and is likely

to remain with us as long as human communities and individuals are anything like we now know them to be. So the central human issue that generates the problematic to which theology addresses itself is likely to have—unhappily—a very bright future ahead of it.

Whether this means there will be a continuing vocation for *theologians*—for those who attempt to address this issue with the aid of the symbol "God," bequeathed to us by the Judeo-Christian tradition—whether there will be a continuing vocation for such theologians over the long haul ahead, I cannot say. Doubtless that depends upon many factors—sociological, economic, religious, moral, and intellectual. In short, it depends on the kind of society and culture, the kind of human beings, we become; and who is in a position to prophesy with conviction on that issue, in this time of great cultural and religious confusion and of rapidly accelerating social change in directions unknown to any previous human experience and history? I will venture to say, however, that if theologians really do address themselves persistently and with insight to the issue of God and the idols, they will be performing a very important service to continuing human self-understanding, whatever might be future social and cultural and religious developments. It is surely, then, a reasonable hope that there will continue to be a significant place for theology as a vocation in human affairs, for theology as a public vocation, whether that vocation is conducted within the institutional setting of church or university or in some other context.

There are many senses in which theology might be conceived to be a vocation. Most of these, perhaps, I have ignored or dismissed, in this address. That is not because I do not regard the service of the church, or the holding of an academic position, or the editing of journals, or the writing of books and articles as valuable. These activities are very important indeed; without them theology probably could not exist at all. But none of these in themselves define what it is that makes a vocation specifically theological; all these activities may be carried on in a nontheological way, even when the name of God is piously invoked. It is when the issue of God and the idols has become the central concern of one's work that theology has truly become one's vocation.

It is not for any of us to sit in judgment on others with regard to the question of who is really a theologian. It is for each of us who aspires to this calling to search out the idols before whom we continue to bow down, and set our minds and hearts once again on the proper work of our vocation.

5

Theology as the Construction of Doctrine

THEODORE W. JENNINGS, JR.

I once defined theology as reflection upon a mythos: that is, as reflection upon those narratives, ritual acts, legal codes, poetic and artistic expressions which, taken together, function as the paradigm for the representation, orientation, communication, and transformation of existence in the world for a religious community.[1] By means of this definition I sought to emphasize that theologies are specific to religious communities—there is or may be Christian theology, Jewish theology, Hindu theology, Buddhist theology, and so on, but not theology in general. Moreover, I had hoped in this way to make clear that theology, and in particular Christian theology, has as its immediate data not the Sacred, God, or Word of God, but images, symbols, narratives, and rituals which mediate or purport to mediate this more ultimate object. Thus theology is ineluctably tied to and dependent upon the various expressions of the religious imagination.

I want now to put forward a second thesis: that the proximate object of this reflection in Christian theology is the critical formulation and reformulation of doctrine. The motives for and thus longer-range goals of this reflection may be understood in a variety of ways: we may hope thereby to reform the church, to make Christianity credible to those outside the church, or to challenge structures of oppression in the world. In general terms, the aim of theological inquiry may be best formulated in terms of the quest for truth, the truth about ourselves, or the world, and thus the truth of God. However these further goals of theological reflection are understood, the immediate goal of theological reflection, the means to these larger ends, is the critical reformulation of doctrine.

There are undoubtedly a great many tasks that clamor for the attention of the contemporary Christian theologian in the academy. There are the tasks associated with the critical interpretation of competing theologies which derive from the dialogical character of theological reflection. There are the immense tasks of clarifying basic principles and investigating the underlying presuppositions of theological inquiry which activate the methodological preoccupation characteristic of contemporary academic theology. There are as well the questions of the relationship between theological perspectives and those represented by other disciplines in the academy. There is the pressing question of the relation of Christianity to other religious traditions and communities and the no less pressing need to relate theological work to the various crises of culture and society. No one could doubt the importance of these tasks. Yet the central task apart from which the others are superfluous, unintelligible, and empty is that of the clarification and critical reformulation of doctrine. If this task is not vigorously pursued, then there are no proposals to be critically examined, no presuppositions to be investigated, no employment of methods however sophisticated, nothing to relate to other disciplines, other religions, other voices in culture and society.

In order to clarify this thesis and, I hope, make it more persuasive I will attend to three interrelated issues. First, what is doctrine and why is it that this is of central importance for the theologian? Second, what is the attitude toward doctrine taken by the theologian? Here I will maintain that the theologian is distinguished from the ecclesial hierarch by an inquiry into the truth of doctrine and thus by a critical reformulation of doctrine. Finally, I will ask how this activity is to be located within the academy, the community of faith, the world.

The Question of Doctrine

That a religious tradition and community should engage in reflection upon its characteristic narratives, cultic acts, legal formulas, and symbolic expressions is by no means self-evident. Indeed, we know that a great many religious groups give no evidence of such activity. That this reflection should take the form of an inquiry into doctrine, should aim at the clarification and/or reformulation of doctrine, is also not self-evident. Yet it does appear that for Christianity at least the formulation and reformulation of doctrine is not an accidental but a characteristic mode of its self-expression.

It is necessary to remind ourselves of this curious feature of Christianity, since we so often fall under the provincial illusion that all religious communities have an impetus toward the formulation of doctrine even if they are not in full possession of a comprehensive body of doctrine. Thus we may speak of Jewish, Moslem, or even Buddhist doctrine and so prevent ourselves from noticing that doctrine (and thus theology) has by no means the same role, place, or incentive in these traditions which it has in Christianity. Thus it is quite possible to think of a fully articulated Judaism in which the formulation of doctrine plays no role or in which it is understood as an aberration from Midrashic or Halakic modes of reflection. The same may also be true, although I am less certain of this, in Islam. But any attempt to understand Christianity without reference to doctrine, whether we think here of christological and Trinitarian controversies, or of the emergence of Scholasticism, or of the professorial reformulation of doctrine and practice associated with the Reformation and Counter-Reformation, would of necessity be self-stultifying. Of course we need also to be reminded, especially in a university setting, that an attempt to understand Christianity only as doctrine apart from cult, folk culture, ecclesial institution, or lived experience is likewise doomed to failure.

We know that other religious traditions, including Judaism, Islam, Hinduism, and Buddhism, do give expression to themselves through the development of reflective-critical discourse, that is, through doctrine by means of theology. It is noteworthy that this often occurs as an apologetic move vis-à-vis an aggressive, perhaps even imperialistic, challenge from Christianity. Thus the development of theology among the major Eastern religious traditions often arises as a response to contact with Christianity. It should be noted that this by no means argues for the superiority of Christianity. Indeed, it is the case that one of the major influences upon the development of Christian theology, especially to be seen in the emergence of Scholasticism, is the contact with a militant and intellectually sophisticated Islam in the eleventh and twelfth centuries.

Having noticed this, we are put on the track of one of the decisive motives for the development of doctrine and thus of the theological reflection that concerns itself with doctrine. We may put it in the form of a thesis: a concern for doctrine emerges within the context of an intellectually vigorous pluralism. Apart from the presence of plural options, a religious tradition may adequately articulate itself through the repetition of cultic acts and the recitation of narratives which together explain and legitimate those features of its corporate life which it judges to be of importance. The need to explain (clarify), defend, and adjust these explanatory acts and narratives arises only where alternatives present themselves. But, of course, not only alternatives. For it is also possible to eliminate alternatives through military force (tribal warfare) or through an appeal to ethnic identity. So one may say: to be an Apache or an American is to say and do as we have said and done. Or the other alternative stories and rituals of the Navaho or the Russians must be extirpated by force, since their mere existence as alternatives must be understood as a threat, as demonic or satanic. It is when ethnicity and force no longer suffice as a response to religious alterity that doctrine is likely to emerge as a basic feature of religious life.

It is a feature which Christianity shares with very few other religious traditions that it emerges in the context of a vigorous religious and intellectual pluralism. The basic terminology of its intellectual life—theology, doctrine, dogma—is taken over from the philosophical schools of the contemporary Hellenistic world, against which it found it necessary to measure itself, with which it was necessary to compete, from which it was necessary to learn. Christianity emerges not in a myth-shrouded past but in the full light of history, at a point which is floodlit with intellectual self-consciousness. Thus the occasion and context of its emergence dictate that Christianity has as one of its characteristic and ineradicable modes of self-expression a doctrinal and theological discourse.

Nor may this be understood as a mere "accident of history" apart from which Christianity might just as well have taken on a different character and discourse. Despite pietistic and liberal disavowals of the Hellenization of Christianity as aberrational, Christianity itself has always maintained that the historical circumstances of its emergence are not accidental but are expressive of that "fullness of time" upon which hinges its self-understanding as the turning or dividing point in history. So seriously is this maintained that it is taken up into the formulas of its credal self-identification, "I believe . . . suffered under Pontius Pilate. . . ."

Beyond this it is significant that Christianity did not have available to it the usual means to dismiss the challenge posed by alternative perspectives and traditions. An appeal to ethnicity was excluded in principle by the extension of the gospel to the "nations." The emergence of Gentile Christianity could not be seen as incidental or accidental but only as central and constitutive of the character of Christianity itself as soon as the Gentile constituency came to predominate. Its very success as a missionary religion in its earliest history forever undermines every attempt to tribalize its meanings and thus precludes this way of disarming the threat of alternative perspectives.

At the same time, the centrality of the motif of the cross, and thus of its identification with the victim of political force, has rendered permanently problematic any recourse to the military option as a means of eliminating the scandal of competing world views. Of course we all know that Christianity has often embraced a military option (the Crusades, the Inquisition, the wars of confessions, etc.) just as it has, on occasion, embraced an ethnocentric mode of being (think, for example, of Afrikaner Christianity). Yet these attempts have always been inherently unstable, subject to internal critique and contradiction.

Indeed, we may say that in at least one respect Christianity requires a permanent pluralism, for Christianity always exists both subsequent to and alongside of Judaism. Thus Christianity exists in a state of permanent disputation with Judaism in which it must define itself over against, while claiming legitimate inheritance from, its "other." To be sure, this also produces the temptation to understand itself as a new Judaism, a new ethnicity, which then avails itself of force to extirpate the challenge to its legitimacy posed by the continuation of the old Israel, the elder claimant to the divine promise. That in attempting to destroy Judaism, Christianity can only destroy itself is the insight of Karl Barth and is, I believe, the irrefutable "lesson" of the Holocaust.

The situation of pluralism is integral for Christianity also on account of its missional and kerygmatic character. It is a faith which addresses itself to the nations and so must articulate itself in a plurality of cultural, religious, and reflective contexts. It has its identity only in this movement of translation and transformation. It is precisely when Christianity loses this pluralistic setting that it is tempted to become a tribal religion with concomitant appeals to ethnicity and to force. The clearest example of this temptation is to be discerned in the medieval period. It is ironic that in our own era of vigorous pluralism we are so often faced with the temptation to locate normative Christianity in this anomalous situation of a self-contained Christendom, rather than seeing in our own situation a return to the normal and characteristic condition of Christianity and perforce to the doctrinal discourse which is an integral form of self-articulation for Christianity. Where doctrinal discourse did not wholly disappear in the period of the early Middle Ages, it was engendered precisely by the necessity of coming to terms, either with Greek-speaking Christianity or with intellectually vigorous forms of Judaism and, subsequently, Islam. From this point of view, the medieval synthesis must be reckoned "a myth of the scholars" which has had the result of inducing a fortress or sectarian mentality on the part of some theologians who seek to defend Christianity from the loss of a culturally privileged space. This only provokes in other theologians the tendency to throw over doctrinal discourse as hopelessly inappropriate to the altered historical-cultural circumstances in which Christianity now finds itself. The truth is that doctrinal discourse has as its only *Sitz im Leben* the context of an intellectually vigorous pluralism. If that is the context in which we indeed find ourselves today, then it is clear that theology must concern itself, above all, with doctrine.

Already in proposing that doctrine be understood to be an integral mode of Christianity's self-articulation, we have anticipated the task that now lies before us—the specification of doctrine as a recognizable discourse. Both the term and the form of discourse designated by the term "doctrine" are borrowed from the philosophical schools of the Hellenistic world—something no less true *mutatis mutandis* for cultic, mystagogic, or legal forms of language used in the Christian community. The term "doctrine" refers to the explication of a philosophical school's distinctive perspectives upon reality and the forms or styles of life that are supposed to be coherent with these perspectives. It is then a reasonable or intelligible account of the distinctive features of a community or tradition. Like the Judaism of Philo, Christianity appropriates this mode of discourse in an attempt to give an account of the language and action, the narratives and cult of the religious community. The account to be given is one that is generally or even universally intelligible and is in this way distinguished from the development of a mystagogic discourse which is concerned with what is by nature secret or esoteric. Without denying that Christianity also developed a mystagogic discourse, its characteristic self-understanding of aiming at all humanity and therefore also the poor, the untutored, prevented the replacement of doctrinal by mystagogic discourse. This doctrinal discourse served the dual role of rendering Christianity intelligible to its own adherents (as catechesis) and of answering objections to its beliefs and practices which came from the world outside the community to which the community's distinctive proclamation was aimed (apologetics). In principle, no final distinction can be made between these two aims since in both cases the goal is an intelligible account of the community's language and practice.

But to understand doctrine in this way is already to introduce a provisional distinction between doctrinal discourse and the religious discourse of which it is, or seeks to be, a generally intelligible account. Doctrine is a constructed or second-order discourse; it is not itself proclamation, liturgy, mythic narrative, apocalypse, etc., but is an attempt to give an intelligible account of these. Failure carefully to observe this distinction has often produced catastrophic consequences. This is particularly evident when doctrine is confused with the narrative discourse or the proclamation of which it is a reflective transformation. Thus there is the attempt to make of the creation narrative a "doctrine" which maintains that the world was created in seven days (i.e., the extreme forms of modern creationism) or the development from the same source of a doctrine of "original innocence"—which illegitimately transposes narrative sequence into a doctrinal locus. Even more complex is the relationship between proclamation and doctrine. The former is *ad hominem* and aims at conversion, while the latter is explicative and aims at intelligibility. Proclamation announces and provokes belief (or unbelief), while doctrine is the articulation of understanding (or mis-understanding).

Unlike proclamation (or sacred narrative or cultic rite), doctrine can make no appeal to an external authority but *only* to intelligibility. Yet it is the intelligibility of precisely *this* kerygma, narrative, or liturgy with which it is concerned.

This concern for discursive intelligibility imposes upon doctrinal discourse the necessity of observing the canons of rationality, of clarification and argument, of plausibility and rigor which are appropriate to explicative discourse generally and which have their origin in the philosophical logos of classical Greece. Doctrine is thus the risk that Christianity may come to appropriate expression in terms of this logos, just as Christianity also risks itself in the liturgical-cultic language which it shares with and borrows from other religious communities.

To recognize the distinction between doctrine and the language and action of the faith community it is not enough to speak here of a simple transformation or mirroring (reflection) of the language of the community. Doctrine does not simply mirror in conceptual form the proclamation or narrative or liturgy of the community. It also has a critical, corrective, and normative function over against the community's internal language. Thus one of the principal tasks of doctrinal formulation is that of testing the contemporary language of the community against those norms which it shares with that community. In this connection the definition of a canon of texts plays an especially crucial role. The very historicity of Christianity's founding events—that they occur in a particular time and place in the full light of historical consciousness—makes both possible and necessary the ongoing testing of present practice against the record of the community's earliest self-articulation.

However, the designation of a biblical canon as the norm which doctrine employs to test the life, language, and practice of the community is by no means adequate. It is better to say that doctrinal discourse becomes critical discourse through attention at one and the same time to the definiteness of Christianity's origin and the eschatological universality of the goal or aim. Thus, for example, is it possible to inquire of the life and practice of the community whether it still bears a positive relationship to the witness and fate of Jesus of Nazareth or has it instead allied itself to the religious, legal, and political forces which conspire to crush Jesus and his movement? Similarly, it is possible to ask to what extent the life of community has turned inward upon itself so as to abandon its openness to the radical transformation of all things, including, of course, itself. There are a number of other ways of formulating these critical norms, but in no case can doctrinal discourse avoid the task of a fundamental and permanent critique. To the extent to which it does so it loses its reason for being as a necessary form of the community's life. It is precisely on account of the universal horizon of Christianity's founding kerygma that doctrinal discourse has emerged, that is, that it was necessary to give a generally intelligible account of Christianity in the first place. Thus a reflective and critical discourse is essential to Christianity as such. That Christianity expresses itself not only as a cult and proclamation but also as doctrine makes clear that what is at stake here is the question of truth—not the truth of a tribe but the truth of and for humanity as a whole, always and everywhere.

Accordingly, nothing can be more catastrophic for theology in its concern for doctrinal discourse than for theology to seek to avoid or to deflect this question of truth. Christianity is grounded in the concern for truth—in this orientation to truth. No avoidance of this question even in the name of "revelation" or "religious experience" can be tolerated if theology is to conform to its own norms, foundations, and reason for being. Indeed, it is precisely because it is concerned with the truth, with a universal and transforming or liberating truth, that theology comes to have any place or role in the academy, in the world of discourse, or indeed even in the church.

To be concerned with doctrine, then, is to be concerned with a reflective critical discourse which attempts to give an intelligible account of the community's life, language, and practice and to test the latter against its own internal norm of definiteness and universality. To be a theologian is to acquire a capacity for and facility with this discourse, to be engaged with this task and work. To postpone or avoid this task is to refuse the vocation of the theologian. It is indeed only when and as the work in and upon doctrinal discourse is undertaken that it then becomes intelligible to ask concerning the methodology and the presuppositions of this discourse or to relate it to the discourse generated by other disciplines, world views, or religious communities.

The Critical Reformulation of Doctrine

Thus far I have maintained that the theologian's work and responsibility entail an orientation to and concern for doctrine. But how and with what aim is the theologian to engage this doctrinal discourse? There are, I believe, three major ways in which we may understand the relationship of the theologian to doctrine. The first, and the one that has most often been explicitly claimed by theologians, is that of transmitting or handing on an already-to-hand body of doctrine. This is the model of the magisterium, the catechetical teaching office of the church. The second way of construing the work of the theologian is that of interpreting or adjusting this body of received doctrine so as to make it intelligible in the altered cultural circumstances within which the theologian works. This is the model of the theologian as hermeneut and apologist. A third way of understanding the work of the theologian is to hold that the theologian is responsible for the construction and fundamental reconstruction of doctrine itself. On this view the theologian does not so much receive doctrine as invent or reinvent it. It is this third model which I shall argue is the most appropriate one for understanding the work of the theologian. But because it depends upon the other two models, it will be necessary to clarify them first.

The Transmission of Doctrine

When the theologian functions as a catechist, theological work consists of instructing the uninformed concerning what the community of faith or, at any rate, the consensus of its intellectual leadership has already (always and everywhere) believed, confessed, and taught. Here the training of the theologian is aimed at producing fluency in an already formed discourse so as to enable an accurate or faithful employment of that discourse. Of course the theologian is not here simply reduced to parroting formulas or to rearranging them, although one sometimes gains the impression that this is the case, especially in reading certain scholastic (of both Protestant and Catholic varieties) theologians. Much constructive work needs to be done especially in clarifying what seems murky and in clearing away misunderstandings both inside and outside the community of faith. Moreover, there is the work of building bridges to the intellectual world outside the community so as to render the received body of doctrine at least formally plausible, although this work does not itself, according to this view, in any way alter the body of doctrine itself.

This way of constructing the work of theology has sometimes lent credence to the pejorative use of such adjectives as "doctrinaire" or "dogmatic," although I believe this is unfair. Indeed, this way of understanding theological work is not unlike the way in which the work of educators is generally understood. So, for example, the rationale regularly given for American public school education is that values of a liberal democratic society are inculcated in our youth so as to make them fit for the tasks of responsible citizenship within the social, economic, cultural as well as political community to which they will belong and may contribute. The model of the educator as catechist, of the intellectual as the transmitter of socially maintained values, is one that theology shares with the educational establishment generally. The business of education in church, society, or academy is, to a significant degree, the business of transmitting doctrine.

Nevertheless there are serious limitations to this way of understanding education generally and the work of the theologian in particular. The very work of clarifying, systematizing, and explaining or defending doctrine introduces changes of greater or lesser magnitude in the doctrine itself. Doctrine is not simply inherited as a *depositum fidei*, it is also transformed by the process of being transmitted. Nor is this to be regarded as a misfortune, for if doctrine were merely received from an ever-receding past, it would be fated to become a dead language no longer capable of articulating the life of a living and historical community, still less of giving an intelligible account of that community's life, language, and practice. Thus the model of the theologian as catechist or pedagogue requires supplementation by the model of the theologian as hermeneut.

The Interpretation (and Adaptation) of Doctrine

That Christianity exists in history, that it therefore enters into altered historical circumstances, altered cultural and intellectual contexts, means that it must come to expression in ways not anticipated by its adherents of a millennium, a century, or even a generation ago. That Christianity is a missionary religion means as well that it must take root in heretofore unknown cultures and be communicated and enacted in previously strange or foreign cultural and linguistic idioms. As with any living organism, it must heed the admonition to adapt or die. Yet this adaptation cannot occur at the level of unconscious mutation, for the definiteness of Christianity, most obviously represented by its canon of texts (Scripture), is a constant challenge to recall it to its self-identity in the midst of change and development.

In response to this exigency we may speak of the theologian as one who consciously and deliberately adapts doctrinal discourse to the altered circumstances of the community. Since this work often takes the form of showing how that which came to expression in the texts of the New Testament (or Luther or Aquinas or whomever) may come to expression in this new language and culture, we may call this the hermeneutical model of the theologian's work.

In order to practice theology as hermeneutics it is not enough to acquire facility or fluency in an inherited or traditional doctrinal discourse. One must also be fluent in some of the cultural languages or discourses of one's larger cultural milieu, while at the same time mastering the idiom of the community's normative sources. Whether or not universities need theologians, it is clear that theologians need universities. Perhaps that is why so many universities have been founded by theologians or built around schools of theology.

This mediational, hermeneutical, and revisionist model of theological work certainly corresponds to a significant dimension of the theologian's responsibility—as does the catechetical model. Yet it too may miss something essential. By speaking of mediation and revision we may be led to forget that the doctrinal discourse to be revised is itself a product of theological construction. Even the biblical text to which appeal is so easily made represents by no means a clear consensus, a single articulation, a simple canon or norm, but a contentious and diverse set of discourses and points of view. Like Luther or Aquinas or even Luke or Paul, the theologian must accept responsibility, not only for the revision but for the construction of doctrinal discourse.

The Construction (and Deconstruction) of Doctrine

At least since the publication of Abelard's *Sic et Non* it has been impossible to suppose that there is a single explicit formulation of doctrine common to the theologians of the Christian community. Although this recognition may be temporarily deflected by the identification of one theologian as the *doctor ecclesia* (not only Aquinas but also Luther and Calvin and even Wesley have been accorded this status by various ecclesial and theological traditions), yet in the end we are brought up against the sheer variety and disparateness of theological and doctrinal judgment. In our own day of ecumenical dialogue this recognition of plurality has extended itself to the relativizing of the hard-and-fast distinction between heterodox and orthodox and has even extended to the recognition of diversity in the New Testament itself. The fracturing of the *consensus fidei* into a series of contending "theologies" has important consequences for our understanding of the work and responsibility of the theologian.

I earlier maintained that doctrine is a constructed discourse. By this I meant to emphasize that doctrine is the product of theological work. It is the product of the attempt to give an intelligible and critical account of the life, language, and action of the Christian community. It is a product and not simply a datum, a result and not just a given; it is constructed and not merely received. While theologians do not generate doctrinal discourse *ex nihilo*, they must again and again construct doctrine *de novo*. If the catechetical model of theology is taken to be essentially and in the proper sense conservative and the hermeneutical model is revisionist or liberal, then the model of theological work I am now proposing would properly be understood to be radical. Yet I take it to be a description of theological work which corresponds to the actual responsibility of theology not only in the modern or postmodern context but in previous eras of theological work as well. Since this aspect or aim of theology is so often overlooked or reduced to silence, it will be necessary to give it somewhat greater attention.

That the theologian has the responsibility to "invent" doctrine is a thesis which can be demonstrated from the history of that discourse we call theology. Whether we think here of the invention of the doctrine of the "image of God" by Gregory of Nyssa, the doctrine of the Holy Spirit by Athanasius and Basil, the doctrine of original sin by Augustine, or any number of similar doctrines, we must reckon with a fundamental transformation of doctrinal discourse— a transformation which like a volcanic eruption fundamentally alters the landscape and both destroys and constitutes its geography. To be sure, this invention, construction, or creation of doctrine does not occur *ex nihilo*. It occurs within and against a discourse or in the conjunction or collision of previously unrelated discourses. Thus the collision of Christianity with Gnosticism, Neoplatonism, Stoicism, Islam, Aristotelianism, is the occasion for the creation of doctrine. Of course many other forms of discourse than doctrine may be generated in this way, but for now it is enough to see what happens here.

One may object that the doctrines I have mentioned were already implicit in the canonical discourse of the community. Do we not find there talk of image of God, of sin, of spirit, and so on? Indeed we do. But not doctrine. We have narratives, bits of liturgy, partial arguments, and so on, in which we may discover here and there the antecedents of doctrinal discourse. But also many "anticipations" which never become doctrine. Why a logos Christology instead of the more widespread angel Christology? Why image of God which occurs so infrequently? Why a pneumatology instead of a sophiology or a dynamology? By a process very like what Lévi-Strauss has called "bricolage," terminology specific to limited and concrete discourse—this narrative, these poems—is given a categorical function and made to organize an entire field of discourse. Ultimately the narrative poem of Genesis 1 comes to be read as an illustration of the doctrine of the *imago Dei* and so acquires a position of privilege scarcely warranted by the preeminence of its location in Scripture as a whole. The same holds true of, for example, the prologue to John's Gospel. If we are to understand the character of doctrinal discourse, we must train ourselves to look beyond and behind the self-evidence of this selectivity and the "obviousness" of this move from poetic or narrative discourse to categorical and explicative discourse or the reflective-critical deployment of this language.

We are assisted in this recognition of the non-self-evidence of doctrinal formulation if we attend to ways in which these formulations are at first so often rejected by the communities to which they are addressed. That Aquinas is the *doctor ecclesia* is self-evident to late-nineteenth-century Catholicism, but many of his most characteristic theses were condemned as heretical by his contemporary community. The innovations of Anselm were condemned by Bernard of Clairvaux, Basil developed the doctrine of the third person of the Trinity in response to his repudiation as a liturgical innovator, and today Barth's doctrine of election must certainly be regarded as far more "heretical" than Schleiermacher's Christology. Doctrinal discourse is generated as an innovation, a reversal, a transgression. It is the fate of such innovations, reversals, and transgressions that they subsequently come to be taken as "orthodox," as indeed the standards of orthodoxy, and so become self-evident. But the theological work itself is never self-evident; it is invariably a transgression of the boundaries and rules of received discourse. How, indeed, could it be otherwise for a discourse founded upon transgression, generated by the collapse of the sacred boundaries between the divine and the human, by the acclamation of the Crucified as Lord?

It is this characteristic moment of innovation, reversal, and transgression which situates theology both within and over against its own inherited discourse. Apart from such a received or traditional language no innovation or transgression is possible. Yet apart from such a reversal, innovation, or transgression the language of doctrine becomes a dead language cut off both from that which provokes it and from the situation within which it is to be employed. This is a lesson which Christianity ought to have learned from the destruction of the citadels of mere orthodoxy by the rising tide of Islam.

That theology is a critical discourse must mean that its critique is always directed first of all upon itself—its own discourse. Especially must this critique be directed against that which it takes to be self-evident, that to which it accords privileged and protected status, that which forms its own foundation and presupposition.

Above all, it cannot take for granted that doctrinal discourse is itself sacred or holy, the linguistic abode of the divine. The language of doctrine must be "deconstructed" lest we be bewitched by our own words, possessed by our discourse, imprisoned by our own constructions. To be engaged in theology is to be concerned with truth—truth which exceeds or ruptures, while at the same time provokes, our discourse.[2] Thus the categories of our discourse, the doctrines themselves, must be continually subjected to the most radical and comprehensive critique. This is true of theistic or trinitarian doctrines, of soteriological or anthropological, of ecclesial or sacramental categories. They must be wrenched out of their self-evidence and volatilized if they are to accompany us in our exile and pilgrimage.

But not abandoned. For our task is still the task of doctrine—still the task of giving an account of the life and language of this community insofar as it is the community of faith. Theological proposals, more or less radical reversals or innovations of doctrine, occur within as well as over against a discourse which we must learn to speak before we learn to alter or transform. We will not succeed in constructing categories or elaborating doctrines that will be proof against the temptation to take them to be "transcriptions of reality" (Owen Barfield) and so as idols. This temptation accompanies any discourse—not only the theological varieties—as Jacques Derrida has shown. Not by abandoning doctrinal discourse but by its deconstruction, its critical reconstruction, will we best attest to the commitment to a truth which shatters all idols and liberates from all mystifications and self-deceptions—a truth therefore which we cannot transcribe but which always provokes our speaking and writing.

The work of constructing or deconstructing or critically reconstructing doctrine is a risky one. The shelters of tradition and authority which protect both catechetical and revisionist modes of theological reflection are not available to the work of construction. Here instead is the task of a responsible freedom. No heaping up of authorities, proof texts, or dogmatic axioms will suffice here, for what is at stake is the truth of these formulations, the truth to which these formulations have attempted to give expression. Nor will it do simply to accommodate this tradition to an altered cultural context, for here again the capacity of this context to be the bearer of

truth is in question and fundamentally in question. To use a met-
aphor familiar to early Christianity, the theologian is like a witness
in open court. Here there is no chance to deflect the question of
the intelligibility, reliability, or veracity of her or his account of that
which both provokes and challenges the life, language, and action
of the community of faith. No appeal to authority will rescue one,
for it is the truth of such putative authorities which is at stake here.
Of course all Christian existence has this character of witness or
testimony. But the theologian has the special responsibility of giving
this account within the sphere and domain of doctrinal discourse—
within the sphere, that is, of an intelligible, public, and reasoned
account.

Theology and the Church

The work of theology as I have described it is by no means always
welcomed in the church. In the name of the primacy of religious
experience, of the life of worship, or of simple obedience, the theologian is often chastised for an excessive preoccupation with the
sphere of language, of reason, of abstraction, and of speculation.
This is even true when this preoccupation has a catechetical or even
scholastic character and form. Thus Melanchthon could exclude even
christological and Trinitarian themes from early versions of his *Loci
Communes*, and Spener in his *Pia Desideria* decried a dogmatic
theology which has lost its rooting, if indeed it ever had any, in
simple and earnest piety. How much more questionable, then, is
the work of the revisionist, liberal, or hermeneutical theologian who
seems always too ready to concede treasured formulations, to accept
an alien "spirit of the time," and thus to exchange a Christian identity
for a "modern" one. Yet the tension between theology and the
church approaches a state of final crisis when the work of theology
is understood to be not only the transmission and interpretation of
doctrine but its construction and deconstruction or critical reconstruction, for here the theologian appears to turn against the community, to challenge openly its inheritance, to raise the question of
truth.

Yet precisely for the reasons that cast greatest suspicion upon
theology it may and must be recognized as a necessary, even if
occasionally challenging or even painful service to the community

of faith. Faith that hopes to distinguish itself from superstition and credulity, that knows or wants to know the difference between false gods and the true God, to abolish the former and cling only to the latter, cannot avoid the intellectual, reflective, and critical work of doctrinal formulation. This will by no means become its only mode of expression, supplanting liturgy, proclamation, or contemplation, but it will always be a necessary one. Similarly the work of translation, revision, and accommodation must be undertaken if the community is to carry out what it takes to be its commission—to go into all the world—to be understood, really understood, by those to whom it addresses the news with which it is entrusted. But it is especially the work of critical reconstruction of doctrine, the open responsible freedom and free responsibility of theological work which is important to the life of the community. For only in exposing itself unreservedly to the question of truth is it possible for the community to serve its commission to be not judge of the world but witness in the world to the truth which banishes all fear, all bondage, all illusion and self-deception.

Theology and the University

But if theology is a necessary and integral task of the Christian community, can it have any place in the academy? Does its churchly character not render it unacceptably sectarian and authoritarian? It must be admitted that there have been theologians and perhaps still are theologians who give the impression that in order to exist, theology must subdue, deflect, or suppress critical reflection, free inquiry, and open discussion. Yet I believe this to be a complete misunderstanding of theological work and responsibility.

Even if we were to restrict the work of theology to that of the transmission and clarification of doctrine, we would scarcely conclude that this work has no place in the modern academy. As I have already suggested, much of the work that is carried out in the university may be understood in precisely this way—as the handing on of a discourse that articulates basic values, orients thought and conduct, and seeks to make it possible for students to understand their life and world. Of course, for its part the academy has the right and the obligation to insist that claims of intelligibility be scrutinized here as elsewhere.

Beyond this, the work of the theologian as hermeneut is one that, far from excluding the theologian from the academy, has in fact founded and fostered the institution of the university from medieval to modern times. If the university is committed to interdisciplinary dialogue, to the task of understanding a variety of discourse, to the ideal of unrestricted communication, then the work of the theologian may not only find a home here but also must do so.

But the work of theology is more than catechetical, more than hermeneutical. It is also the work of critical inquiry and responsible formulation. It is to be characterized by an unreserved commitment to truth. Theology cannot claim to be in possession of the truth, but it is provoked and driven by the question of truth. Its discourse is the attempt to respond to this provocation, to give an account of it, and to submit this account to open and full discussion and decision. The theologian as theologian must be at war with falsehood, self-deception, and mystification and in this struggle joins in friendly competition with both the natural and the human sciences.

Conclusion

It is a commonplace that theology exists between Jerusalem and Athens, in the tension between church and university. Yet in truth, theology, like the Christian community, has taken up its abode neither in Jerusalem nor in Athens but in Rome. The Rome of the Hellenistic world, like the New York, Moscow, Paris, Cairo, Peking, or New Delhi of today, was at the heart of the cultural, political, and economic life of the world. The eschatological hope of the Christian community is not that God will found the church or even the university but that earth and heaven will be transformed. Theology can no more be a merely academic exercise than it can be a merely ecclesial one. Its formulations, its intelligible account, its critical reflection are directed not only to the church and the academy but to the world. The truth to which it commits itself is truth which abolishes fear and illusion, and sets free. Its aim is not merely to understand the way things are but to attest to the transformation wrought by the One who promises, "Behold, I make all things new." To be concerned with theology is to be concerned with theory, to be sure, but a theory of liberating praxis.

Books of theology will not feed the hungry nor heal those lamed in the torture houses of this world nor give justice to the despised and dispossessed. Compared to deeds of liberating power, theology is an unimportant work. Yet it is the work of the theologian. And it may play some small role in this larger and more important work. In common with other disciplines, it may engage in the work of banishing illusion or interrogating claims to self-evident necessity, of exposing idolatry and ideology. It may also serve by giving an account of our hope, of that by virtue of which we resist resignation to the way things are, or the idolatrous celebration of the status quo. If we only succeed in giving an understandable account of what it might mean to hope and not despair, to persevere in hope rather than resort to the weapons of violence and fear, we will have served well not only church and university but our world as well.

NOTES

1. *Introduction to Theology: An Invitation to Reflection Upon the Christian Mythos* (Philadelphia: Fortress Press, 1976).

2. *Beyond Theism: A Grammar of God-Language* (Oxford: Oxford University Press, 1985).

6

Theology as the Interpretation of Faith for Church and World

LANGDON GILKEY

Let me begin our thoughts on the vocation of the theologian with the realistic distinction between the glorious possibilities of that task and the actuality of its embodiment. When I was in graduate school at Union, we rightly took it for granted that the vocation of any theologian worth his or her salt was to address the whole church about the faith and to speak the Christian word to the world, and we assumed therefore that theologians in fact did this. After all, had not Reinhold Niebuhr not only dominated the last World Council of Churches meeting but also addressed regularly the CIO, and had not Paul Tillich spoken to a hushed American psychoanalytic society, not to mention the assembled "greats" who had graced the covers of *Time* magazine? Needless to say, it did not take long for some of us more ordinary mortals to realize that the full embodiment of our common task is rare indeed and far beyond our reach. I am lucky to speak once in a while to, say, Nebraska's Methodist ministers or to a group of concerned laity in a local church! Full embodiment of our task comes only with the providential gift of near-genius; but still the task is constant and stands as a challenging, if unrealized, possibility, even for each of us. It is of the full structure of this task, not of the limitations that our own meager talents set on our enactment of it, that I wish here to speak.

Not surprisingly, the only grounds for envisioning, shaping, defining, and limiting the task of the theologian are themselves *theological*. Thus we must start with two theological assumptions that set, for me, the contours of the theologian's vocation. Both concern God and the manifestation or presence of God; it is from the modes of that presence that the theological task of declaring, interpreting, and elaborating that presence and its implications takes its shape. The first assumption that creates the community of the church and so theologians as well is that God is present decisively and for us men and women fully through the life and work, past and present, of Jesus who is the Christ. It is here that the community of the church finds its empowering center. It is here too that individual Christian life and Christian theology find their source and center, their most significant authority, standard, and commission, that on which and by which the first, Christian existence, lives and that of which the second, Christian theology, primarily speaks. The second assumption is that God is also manifested, as an unconditional and ultimate creative presence, in the world and thus in culture, as the source or ground of creativity, of judgment, and of new possibility in ongoing historical life. It is, I think, simply biblical to affirm that social and cultural life also stand *coram Deo*—in the presence of God—in history, and thus, in however dim or distorted a fashion, does that cultural life represent a response to the continued divine presence creating, preserving, and directing finite being. As there is a *cultural* side to the presence of God in Christ in the church, so there is a *religious substance*, a dimension of ultimacy in every communal and cultural whole.

While they are very different and should be carefully distinguished, these two modes of the divine presence, in church and in culture, are inseparable, deeply intertwined, and interdependent— as both the Old Testament account of Yahweh's presence to Israel *through* history and its events and the eschatological goal of the kingdom uniting covenant community with the redeemed world make clear. The task of the church—that is, of the grace and truth promised to it—is in large part the support, criticism, and healing of the world as well as of itself in the world. No theological or sermonic expression of the church's message is possible except it embody as well as reshape the forms of thought and value of its culture. The inner religious life of each of us, the forms of our anxieties, our sins, our deepest loyalties and hopes, is shaped by our outer world: by the structures of our social world and by the events that transpire there. Inner and outer, personal and social existence create and re-create each other, inner creativity and courage resulting continuously in new outer structures and new solutions to outer problems, but also the present sins of our hearts warping the historical institutions we do shape into a hard, semipermanent objective fate for our children and our children's children. No church can exhibit the presence of God if it ignores the sins and injustices of its community; it loses its own inner soul, its religious substance, when it loses touch with its task of criticism and of healing in its own world. Then it becomes merely its world blessing its community's injustices and encouraging its community's aggression— as did the German churches and as may again the American churches. The message of the church has thus, through no accident, a dual focus: Christ *and* his kingdom. We are called to deal both with sin and with the outer social results of sin, with self-interest, pride, and greed *and* their consequences on the historical fatedness of rapacious and oppressive institutions, unjust and exploitative social structures, and aggressive communities. As estrangement from God results in inner distortion and despair and in outer injustice and destruction, so God's creative and redemptive grace and meaning are present in both church and world, in the means of grace and in the creative structures of culture. And from these basic presuppositions about the divine presence and about human need, theology derives its task and the theologian his or her vocation.

The theologian therefore has a dual role, churchly and public, on the boundary between church and world, as Tillich put it, at home and yet not quite at home in either one. In both, the theologian has a vocation and a message, but in neither church nor world can that message be uncritical, undialectical. The theologian's churchly role—when he or she seeks the ear of the church—is not fulfilled by an uncritical proclamation of the American world around the church, nor is it fulfilled by an unchallenged championing of the church to itself as the light of its world. Hence the theologian is, as is the minister, uneasy *in* the church. Correspondingly, the public role of the theologian—when he or she seeks the world's ear— must also be paradoxical, dialectical, and thus uncomfortable. A continued defense of ourselves as the church to the world, of the church as a significant institution, or of God as a rational idea among other rational ideas, and of theology as "a respectable discipline," a defense conducted on the world's terms and according to its criteria, is far too insignificant a theme, is not only defensive but a bit narcissistic, and, by submitting the Christian message to the barren standards of the world without a struggle, it tells the world little it does not already know. What our role may be in the church and in the world will be the subject of the rest of our remarks. For the moment, one implication of our argument is that, in contrast to Van A. Harvey, it is for me no accident that from the beginning theology has resided—albeit only with a temporary lease!—in *both* church and academy, in the world's universities as well as in the church's seminaries. Theology is, as Tillich showed, a compound both of message and of cultural situation, and so it needs both—and, as we have noted, it speaks to both. But it is also true that this theological compound, when true to itself, represents a bitter as well as a healing prescription for both of the institutions (church and university) that bear the necessary elements of that compound and that alternatively house its practitioners.

The major role of the theologian is clear enough: it is to produce relevant, contemporary, and appropriate constructive theology and to present this to the Christian community. Its job is, therefore, to reflect on the Christian message in relation to the human situation, personal and social, and in the light of the present cultural situation. This task of theology can be defined in two ways: it presents an understanding of contemporary human existence as that existence is interpreted through the symbols of the Christian tradition, or, alternatively, it presents a contemporary interpretation of Christian faith in its relation to human existence. It sets into contemporary conceptual form the Christian gospel as that gospel addresses, challenges, and heals the personal and social history of men and women. Clearly first of all, then, theology is a function of the church, of the Christian community. It represents that community's effort to *understand* itself and its message, to define what it is in the area of belief, of fundamental conviction, that is to say, what basic symbols or sets of symbols constitute that community, that distinguish it from other communities, and that therefore guide and empower its life, its decisions, its actions and policies, and its rites and customs.

We should note, however, that even in realizing this churchly task of understanding and thus of defining itself—and continually reunderstanding and redefining itself—theology relates itself also to the world. The gospel addresses universal human existence, yours and mine, that of churched and unchurched, of ecclesia and world alike. For the destructive problems that wrack the world on the one hand and the creative meanings that would heal it on the other represent the same problems and the same answers that the gospel pictures. If sin and death are what the gospel as a message addresses, these two do not confine their destructive power to the people who hear the Word, nor are faith and love relevant only for the existence of the churched. A relevant, intelligible, appropriate constructive theology is thus not only a necessity for the church's life, it also represents an important message for the world, an interpretation of our common existence which the world might well heed to its benefit and so which must be presented to the world with the same seriousness it is presented to the church.

Theology is a reflective task. Its goal is understanding, understanding through a valid *theory*, shaped by Christian symbols, of the nature and problems of human existence, personal and social, of the nature, activity, and promises of God, and thus of the hopes for personal and historical life. To *be* a Christian is to live Christianly, with faith and love, to have one's *existence* characterized by a Christian relationship to God and to others. This is personal and existential, and here all of us are radically equal, for none has more talent for this than do others. Theology and doing theology are significantly different from this. Theology represents a Christian *theory* about existence and the God to whom it is essentially related. It is Christian understanding, and it characterizes our *thinking*, whereas Christian life or faith characterizes our *existence*, the way we are and act. One implication of this distinction is that "wrong" theology does not signal a lower level of Christian existence; nor does a "correct" theology (or one's Ph.D. in theology) signal a higher level of Christian existence. Any one of us can grade a systematic paper or review a theological book; none of us, only the Lord, can grade a neighbor's faith or give a final review to another's religious existence.

Another implication of the distinction between faith and existence on the one hand and theology on the other is that theology relates itself first of all to other *theories* and only indirectly to concrete situations in actual life. It seeks, for example, to clarify the rela-

tionship of the Christian understanding of human being with the
psychological theories of Freud or Piaget; its understanding of history with the views of Toynbee or Marx; its views of knowledge and/
or of reality with those of Whitehead, Heidegger, and Wittgenstein.
It gives understanding, and through that gift it *may* provide inspi-
ration (and possibly may even become a vehicle of new faith and
action). But its primary goal is to help us to *understand* what we
believe: who we are, what our deepest problems are, who God is,
what we believe God has done to reconcile us with one another and
with God, and what we are to do in obedience and out of love.
Preaching proclaims the gospel to particular persons in particular
situations, persons faced with particular problems and obligations,
that is, with regard to their religious existence, their faith and their
love. Theology (even liberation theology) presents an understanding, an interpretation, of the gospel in relation to the human situation generally, and thus in relation to our culture's understanding
of that situation: its relevant sciences, social science, psychology,
historical knowledge, and philosophy. While it is surely true that a
theologian must understand the ups and downs, the absurdities and
pathos, of life and be in touch with his or her own existence and
that of others—else he or she can hardly be creative in theology—
still most immediately he or she must be intellectually conversant
with the *theoretical* interpretation of the human situation (for example, with Marxism) that characterizes contemporary culture. In
any case, it is only in the latter area—in the area of *theories* relative
to theological understanding—that we can hope formally to educate
and to assess or "grade" one another.

The distinction between religious existence and theological reflection on that existence helps us to be clear about the *status* of
theology. It used to be held that the center of valid dogmatic theology was itself revealed, that a sound theologian could therefore
unambiguously "state the faith of the church," and as a consequence
that true theology was absolute, changeless, and universal. Now,
however, we realize that theology is not directly God-given but
represents a *human* response to the divine presence. To be sure,
our commitment, loyalty, and obedience—our religious existence—must be, or should be, unconditional; but we should always
recall that our theology is not. Theological propositions are *our*

reflection on our faith and the revelation that is its object, not propositions revealed in themselves. Thus any given theology is relative and partial, as all our thinking is, *one* perspective on the Christian message, in the present case the perspective of a male, middle-class, white, Protestant, and married American (possibly even Chicagoan) of advanced middle age. If *I* don't recognize this partial and thus relative character to my theology, you may be sure others will: blacks, women, Europeans, South Americans—even misguided colleagues—and if by accident any expert should come across this in a hundred years, he or she would be able to say, even after only one paragraph, "an understanding of theology typical of late-twentieth-century American Protestantism during the decline of the Anglo-Saxon Western world!" To believe that theological truths are absolute, changeless, and universal is to forget that theology represents human thinking, and that all our thinking, even that creative of theology, has a *historical* character. Any particular theology is therefore a *proposal* to the church community, not an authoritarian or dogmatic edict, a proposal for understanding our common faith, a proposal for our consideration about our Christian existence, and thus a proposal to be assessed, criticized, amended, or rejected by each of us and by the community as a whole. Even if there is one Lord, there are many theological points of view pointing toward that one Lord. One does not therefore *believe* in a given theology, even one emanating from Emory or Chicago; one believes in God and God's Word, and holds, or may hold, that a given theology is the best expression for the moment of that which is believed. Let me add that the inevitably parochial, even local, character of our theology does not mean that we should try to write a "male" theology, an "American" theology, a "Southern" theology. We should attempt to point our propositions toward the universal, as proposals about human existence *generally* for the *whole* church's understanding; soon enough their relativity will become evident. But we should not *try* to present only part of the truth.

Granted, then, the theoretical and the relative perspectival character of theology, why is theology important or even necessary for the Christian community, for the church? If constructive theology is not a vocation for everybody in the church—as are faith and works of love—why is it a vocation for anybody? The necessity, it seems to me, is based on the historical, the communal, and the personal character of our faith, and on the transcendent character of God. Christianity is a communal, an interpersonal form of religion. As a message about a historical event rather than a universally available experience, Christian faith is generated not in individual experience but is communicated from one person to another by proclamation, preaching, teaching, and witness or example. As it comes to each of us and is passed on, it is a Word that must first of all be *said* or *declared*. And in order for that to be possible, the message must be thought out, reflected, set into intelligible, coherent, and relevant concepts for it to be spoken, on the one hand, and heard and acknowledged, on the other. Preaching and teaching presuppose a theology, a coherent, unified interpretation of the faith. By the same token, this faith, if it is to have any reality at all, must be personal, assented to by the mind of each one who affirms it. For it to be *ours* at the deepest level of our existence, we must understand its meaning and be assured of its truth, we must be able to think what we believe and so assent to it—if we are to believe it. And if we are to guide our life by it, again we must be able to think it. As do proclaiming and speaking a message, so believing and affirming one presuppose a theology, again a coherent, intelligible, and credible interpretation of the faith. And both reasons call, moreover, for a continually renewed or revised theology, so that the message can be said relevantly and credibly to us and affirmed personally by us with understanding and conviction.

Finally, the transcendence represented by the object of our faith calls for theology in those who receive and acknowledge this transcendence. The message comes to us from beyond ourselves, from beyond our experience and everything that is immediately around us. To be sure, grace is communicated *to* our experience, *in* our liturgies, *through* our sacraments, *through* our preaching, and *through* persons transparent to the divine. But grace is not merely our experience, nor identical with the liturgical rite, a sacramental reality, even a powerful sermon or the most loving person. The divine Word and power communicates itself through each—still each is only a *medium,* and our reception must be pointed *through* the medium to what lies in and also beyond it. In us it is in large part reflection that lifts us up beyond the immediate, the visible, the present medium of grace, that, in other words, makes the divine presence in and through these means into means of *grace*, the divine immanence into what is also the divine transcendence. Correspondingly, though grace is in the church, it also judges the church and so transcends it. Again reflection, and thus theology, is the condition for that dialectical yes and no, for that acceptance of, and yet transcendence over, the immediate in order that the medium be a true symbol of grace. Thus because of the historical, the communal, and the personal character of Christian faith, and because of the transcendent character of the God of faith, theological reflection is a necessary component in the life of the community. That community must understand that which it believes and that by which it guides its life, and that striving toward understanding culminates in and is represented by the vocation of the theologian.

It is evident that for theology to perform this necessary function in the Christian community, it must be *polar* in character. On the one hand, it must express the original and central message of the faith and thus point us beyond our immediacy in our cultural present to God's presence in the event of Jesus Christ and subsequently in the means of grace related to that event. On the other hand, it must bring that message to us, to our understanding and our modes of thinking, and thus express that message in a form intelligible, credible, and relevant to us—that is, in the form of modern concepts, categories, standards, and aims. If it is too orthodox, too time-honored and thus timeless, theology will enshrine a message addressed to another day than our own, a message that may evoke nostalgia but will not penetrate into our personal being as relevant to our existence here and now. If it is too timely, it will merely repeat the world's wisdom, and failing to communicate anything new and healing to our world, it will leave us again untouched. Constructive theology is, therefore, an infinite risk: the tradition must be revised and set into modern categories lest it not be heard at all. But it must also transform those categories into *Christian* form—into a Christian interpretation of contemporary experience—lest no message be there. If we merely re-present tradition, we lose our touch with the world and with ourselves; if we merely re-present our world, we lose the message—here lies the double risk. We see, then, how important it is that there be a *variety* of constructive theologies and that each recognize itself as a *proposal* to the church community. For each new theological construction represents a creative reinterpretation and thus an infinite risk, a risk to be assessed in openness, in critical judgment, and in infinite interest by the community.

The fundamental task of theology is therefore that of revision, of re-presentation. With the obfuscation characteristic of any profession, we now term this the "hermeneutical" problem, the problem of interpreting what was said or written in one age into the categories and concepts of our own age, or as Tillich called it, the union of the eternal message with the cultural situation characteristic of our time and place. There is no question that this hermeneutical enterprise defines the constructive task and thus that the hours recently spent pondering its problems and the pages used explicating its method have been necessary and well used. If we seek to do constructive theology, each of us has to formulate as carefully as possible a procedure for this translation or revision, and to test that procedure against the often polite but more frequently horrified rejection of our colleagues.

At this point, however, we encounter the present temptation lying in wait for the contemporary theologian, especially one in a major university graduate school. This is the temptation to linger so long in the preparatory enterprise of hermeneutical method, of answering the question of how to go about doing theology, that the theologian never in fact realizes, re-presents, or reexpresses a single aspect of the original message. Let us remember that a modern and contemporary method of constructive theology, however brilliant it may be, is not itself the gospel or even a modern, contemporary reinterpretation of the gospel, and that the problems that a method of theological inquiry faces in the academic community are not the same as the problems that wrack and threaten to destroy the world's existence. Thus, doing theological method is not yet doing theology, however much it may seem in academia that the two are one and the same. As with getting in shape, the concentration on method is important and necessary, but it is not the same as running the race that must be run. To repeat, the central "churchly" task of the theologian is to re-present the Christian gospel—that is, the full set of Christian symbols—as an interpretation of our common, human existence; and to re-present this in a form appropriate to its original sources and intelligible and credible to contemporary minds. Thus can theology aid the community of the church in reshaping its own life—its own "religious substance"—closer to a genuine Christian substance. For only in this way can that community become (like its Lord) a symbol, a medium, a sacrament of grace to its world.

The primary task of the theologian is the revision of the Christian message in contemporary terms, a message addressed, of course, first of all to the community of the church which seeks to live by that message. The corresponding temptation of the theologian (now that we have lost all power in the world; there were many other temptations before that power slipped away from us!) is so to concentrate on that hermeneutical task, and especially the interesting, alluring intellectual problems connected with it, that the message itself and especially the relevant, biting, healing relation of that message to ourselves and to the world cease to be central objects of reflection. The gospel, we have said, contains a Christian message to and about human existence; it presents an interpretation of our common existence that is both true about it and healing to it. It is therefore addressed to the world and not alone to the saints, judging, challenging, shaking, healing, and transforming the world. Correspondingly, while the primary requirement for any theology is that it be a re-presentation of the message to the church, it is no less also necessary that it be a re-presentation to our world, to the cultural and social life of men and women in our time.

In our remarks so far we have cited a number of reasons why this last point is important. Let us summarize them in a slightly new fashion and thus with a somewhat new emphasis. First of all, the church, and therefore the message to the church, cannot be separated from the world around it. If it seeks to do that, the church fools itself about itself and thus loses itself in a morass of self-deception. The anxieties and fears that bother and threaten the listeners in our pews are the world's problems: unemployment and inflation; disease, age, and death; loneliness and conformity; anxiety about public violence and racial conflict; fear of nuclear war and of national weakness; anxiety about our way of life in relation to the world's future—and so on and on. Thus in addressing *our* own anxieties as Christians in church, we are in fact discoursing on our wider culture's problems. If we would understand our personal crises, therefore, we must as theologians understand also that wider structure; if we would speak a healing word to personal problems, we must envision new possibilities for our cultural history. To separate personal problems relevant to religion from social problems relevant only to political and economic policy is to divide us up artificially; it is *we* who suffer from both sorts of problems, and we who seek to deal with them. Thus, correspondingly, if we seek to solve our personal economic and social problems either by drink or by an inordinate ambition, we are enacting and embodying a wider social problem. If we attempt to resolve our economic and social anxieties by anti-Semitic or white racist attitudes and actions, even more are we embodying and spreading a social disease. And finally, if we think to ease our fears for America's security by amassing unlimited nuclear arms, by electing to support friendly dictators, or by commandeering all the natural resources we can, we have *ourselves* incarnated, joined, or *become* the forces of destruction rampant in our world—in effect, voluntary instruments of a scourge in modern history.

Personal crises tempt us to individual sins. In much the same way—though perhaps obscured by their size—social crises represent not just political and economic problems or puzzles. They also bring with them moral crises and they demand moral decisions. They make us deeply anxious and tempt us, only now all of us *together*, as a community, to attitudes of self-concern and to acts of selfishness: of expropriation, of aggression, of violence. The German church was silent in the face of deep social, economic, and political crises, and it remained craven before the demonic reactions of its community to those crises; likewise, much of the American church has been silent in the face of racial division and nationalistic expansionism. Both made evident that a church which ignores the injustices and the upheavals in its immediate world ends by becoming *part* of them, an instrument of them, and so corrupts itself endlessly—and it makes of its message, however sublime, an "ideology" justifying that sordid historical reality. Let us recall that it is only the *sinners* in a given historical situation that ignore social sins, that try to be indifferent to the injustices of the world they rule and profit from: to the masters, the oppressors and the aggressors, social sins of inequality, of injustice, and of imperialism seldom have relevance to their private religion! Those who suffer from these acts, however, those who are sinned *against*, the oppressed, slaves and servants, the dominated and the persecuted, the hungry, do not regard that worldly situation as religiously indifferent or even as unrelated to the divine judgment.

The gospel can hardly *be* the gospel if it does not address the ills that beset us and the sins with which we seek to escape those ills. And those ills and those sins are, for any church community, the sins of its own social world, nothing else. Thus for the gospel to challenge, judge, heal, and transform, it must relate itself, not just to the contemporary church, not just even to cultural theories and to cultural self-understanding; it must relate itself also to the social structures of destruction and of possibility in that historical world, to its economic, its political, its class, its racial, and its national developments. It is no accident that the gospel is a gospel for persons *in* community, for inner individuals *in* their social roles, for personal commitment and decision *in* the wider kingdom. As a consequence, a theological interpretation of that gospel must include the theoretical *and* the practical relationship of the gospel to the world's life, to its crises and its political meanings, to the total life of contemporary history.

There is another point in this regard significant for the wholeness of theology as a contemporary expression of the Christian message. The primary task of theology, the hermeneutical task, represents the effort to unite our message from the past to the intellectual, social, moral, and political characteristics of our cultural world. For theologians acutely conscious of the anachronistic character of their tradition, its pseudoscience, its literalism, its frozen immobility and dogmatism—even its pallid humanitarianism and its male bourgeois prejudices—the task of hermeneutics unwittingly encourages the assumption of the stability, the credibility, and the viability of the modern culture to which it seeks to adapt the gospel. The gospel that we bring often seems to us precious but precarious, barely acceptable by the world's hardheaded wisdom. Whether this attitude is more true for theologians in academia somewhat nervously present in the self-assured atmosphere of an academic council, made up of prestigious scientists, sociologists, and psychologists, or of preachers trying to communicate to a committee of important and self-confident bankers, brokers, manufacturers, and labor leaders, I will not say. In either case, the first task of theology, the revisionary task, is apt to encourage a serious misunderstanding of the gospel and a vast illusion about the stability and viability of the world to which it is now addressed.

For the simple fact of our present is that the contemporary world to which we rightly seek to adapt the gospel is, if anything, in *worse* shape than is either the gospel or the church that proclaims it. It is probably more anachronistic and illusionistic, it is a good deal more threatened from the outside, and it seems bent on a path of self-destruction even more than do the forces of traditional religion. This is not to state that modern Western culture, and with it the American way of life as its latest edition, is necessarily on the de-cline—no one knows that much about even the immediate future. It is to state that culture faces serious internal and self-generated difficulties, even contradictions, and that the precariousness of its present dominance and, through that, the precariousness of its con-tinued life have revealed themselves with increasing clarity in our generation. A sophisticated industrial society has begun to develop economic problems of inflation and of supplies and social problems of urban decay which it never dreamed possible; a technological industrial society, fated to an uncontrollable expansion, seems to be doomed shortly (by, say, the year 2000) to consume the resources on which it must live and to destroy the nature system through and in which it must exist. Meanwhile let us recall that dominant power was long resident among the Western nations alone—the last time a non-Western power threatened or could threaten the West was in 1456, five hundred years ago, when the Turks stormed Vienna! Such dominant power in our lifetime has fled the West and is now beginning to manifest itself elsewhere. Only one of the four major world powers is now Western. And if you don't think America feels this precipitous loss in anxiety, puzzlement, frustration, and panic, then just listen. Correspondingly, like many an aging leader, anxious over the loss of former power, we are beginning to shed the courage of our creative ideals and to retreat to the cynical and eroding interest of mere self-protection. The strident call to forget human rights and prudently to bolster those sorry tyrants who depend on us around the world is a sure sign of anxious weakness rather than of mature strength, of a community that, in fearfully whiffing the dank odor of its own mortality, empties its ideals of all real content in order to save—in order, that is, to endanger more dramatically— its life.

This is our real world. It is grim, it is precarious, and it will not go away. It needs desperately, as does the church, clear under-standing and interpretation, and, above all, judgment, grace, and hope. Merely to adapt the gospel *to* that world is to misunderstand the meaning and the purpose of the divine judgment and of grace, and to harbor vast delusions about that world. Perhaps the most vivid example of theological insight in Christian history, of a vision of what theology might and ought to be, was when Augustine re-alized, just before the demise of the Roman Empire, that the effort, long-honored in the established church, merely enthusiastically to adapt Christianity to that Roman culture—creative, powerful, glo-rious, and eternal as Rome had long seemed—was mistaken, that the Christian vision must *transcend* as well as engage that culture, and that this too was a part of the calling of theology. And in that act of transcendence of the Hellenistic world, as well as of adaptation to it, he sowed the seed of endless new ecclesiastical and cultural possibilities, possibilities by no means yet visible to him as he watched the Vandal hordes circling the walls of besieged Hippo waiting for the kill.

It appears that we are saying that the theologian must know every-thing about present culture, even its probable future, as well as everything about the gospel and its tradition—a large order indeed. Certainly the theologian's interest and curiosity about our social as well as our personal situations must be wide, for the fire from heaven bursts into light and heat only when it strikes the earth, not before. But we can restrict that demand somewhat. The constructive the-ologian is not and cannot be a specialist in each of the important contemporary disciplines: in the sciences, in economics, in politics, in sociology and psychology. The construction of theories and pol-icies in these areas is not the theologian's responsibility. However, no area of culture is separate from the "religious substance" of the culture, from the effects, theoretical and practical, of that culture's

most fundamental beliefs. There is a central spiritual ethos of a
culture's life that unifies each element and each vocation into a
cultural whole, that gives to each of a culture's sciences and arts its
particular stamp, and that provides standards for its actions and
content to its aims. The economic, political, social, and individual
life of our culture is, for example, permeated by a matrix of crucial
symbols drawn from the hopes and aims of science, of technology,
of democracy, and of capitalism, which together make up what we
call "the American way of life" in all of its facets. This "religious
substance" is a legitimate and crucial object of the theologian's concern, of, that is, the theologian's "theology of culture." To this
"secular mythology," if I may so term it, theological self-understanding must continually relate itself: in analysis, in retrieval and support
of what is creative in that cultural tradition (for much is), in criticism
and judgment of what is false and dangerous, even demonic, there,
and in the promise of grace and of hope for *its* future. For the task
of the church, and thus of theology, in the world is to shape that
cultural religious substance positively closer to a Christian form:
more just, more equal, more compassionate and humane, more
peaceful, and, negatively, to guard it from the self-destruction of
anxiety, of insecurity, of panic, of radical self-love, of sin. Put in
terms of disciplines, systematic or constructive theology, then, is
fulfilled *only* when it is supplemented on the one hand by theology
of culture and on the other by liberation theology. Without them,
constructive theology is apt to collapse into method and remain
formal, academic, unrelated, ineffective, narcissistic, ideological.
Without the theological center of the gospel in relation to our existence, however, theology of culture and liberation theology remain
void of significant criteria or standards and therefore empty of deeper
purpose and hope.

It is an old summation of the gospel—and thus of the task of
theological interpretation—to say, first, that it deals with sin, with
fate, and with death, and second, that it is respectively God's mercy
and grace in Christ that addresses *sin*, God's providential power in
history that overcomes *fate*, and God's eternal being that triumphs
over *death*. All of this is included in the gospel and thus in the task
of theology. In the church, where Word and Sacrament are present
and where the gospel is re-presented, the depths of sin are uncov-

ered and faith and love may be borne. But the world is in the church and the church is in the world. Both the church and world together participate in the estrangement of sin. Both suffer under the fatedness of history: its unjust institutions, its terrifying trends, its destructive and irrational events, its menacing future. And both together face the inevitability of death. To re-present in constructive form the whole gospel means, therefore, to encompass all three: God, ourselves before God, and the contemporary historical situation in which God's power, judgment, and new possibilities are manifest. What is it we need and must know in theology? It is God, the soul, and the world we souls share together—that is all, but it is enough!

7

Theology as Thoughtful Response to the Divine Call

JOHN B. COBB, JR.

As you know, there is widespread sentiment to the effect that Christian theology does not fit the university. I will propose first that theology, far from being inappropriate to the university, provides a model for reform. In the second section I will discuss what that reform would mean for the seminary. In section three I will comment directly on the task of constructive theology, and in the concluding section I will explain how what I have said is influenced by, or embodies, process thought.

I

The contemporary university is structured, it seems, on two principles. Some portions are organized for the purpose of preparing people to do particular jobs in society. The theological school can be justified by this criterion. Other portions are organized on the basis of distinct subject matters. The study of Christian literature and history can be defended on these grounds. A case can also be made for the study of the phenomenon of religion historically, psychologically, sociologically, phenomenologically, and philosophically. There is a real question whether this all belongs in a single department or should be divided among the other departments of the university. But that is not our topic here.

The question here has to do with constructive Christian theology. Can it be justified as a discipline appropriate to the university? This is not a new topic, and, indeed, concern about this matter has already had a profound effect on the self-understanding of theologians.

This is most apparent in central Europe. Whereas the great theologians of earlier times discoursed on many things and felt no need to give a single consistent account of the method they employed, theology as a university discipline has felt the need to define its subject matter and its method narrowly. The tendency has been to understand theology as contemporary interpretation of the Bible, in short, as biblical hermeneutics. In its more professional contexts, theology adds that this interpretation is for the sake of preaching. In this way theology establishes itself as pursuing a distinct task that can constitute it as one department alongside the other university departments—with no threat to them.

This type of self-definition works better in central Europe than in the United States. There it describes what many theologians in fact do. Here it does not. There to some extent the preachers appreciate the help of the theologians. Here most preachers turn to popular psychology and, at best, to the works of biblical scholars. Theologians leave the actual practice of biblical hermeneutics chiefly to biblical scholars, although we may share in discussions about hermeneutical principles. In any case, the restriction of theology to biblical hermeneutics, even when this is quite broadly conceived, would seem much too narrow. But no alternative definition of theology that justifies it as a university discipline is current in American circles.

My proposal is that we set aside concern for university norms in our effort to understand our task as theologians. I propose that we ask instead what it is we are called to do. We are, of course, called to be informed about what other theologians have done and are doing so that we will not work in a vacuum. But this is propaedeutic to work rather than its substance.

I suggest that we are called fundamentally to think about contemporary problems that seem important to us. If we truly are Christians, and if our Christian identity informs our thinking, then in some measure our thinking will be theology. But it is better to limit theology a little more narrowly. When we think theologically we think *self-consciously* as Christians. That is, we are reflective about the way our Christian identity informs our thought.

One reason this rather simple understanding of Christian theology is not widely accepted is that it fits poorly with university expectations. It violates them in two main ways.

First, Christian theology openly acknowledges that it seeks truth from the perspective of a particular identity or tradition. This appears to violate the university commitment to objectivity, neutrality, and open-ended inquiry.

Second, Christian theology understood in this way refuses to limit itself to one particular subject matter that can be distinguished from all other subject matters. It refuses to confine itself in the proper departmental manner.

The suspicion that, however it defines itself, theology will in some such ways violate the norms of the university has rendered it widely suspect. In general it is restricted to theological schools and to their task of professional education.

The one exception in major universities is to be found in seminary-related graduate programs in religion. Even these are often under considerable pressure to downplay "theology" in favor of philosophy of religion, history of religions, and other more academically approved disciplines. But the term "theology" and, to some extent, the discipline itself still survive.

There are analogous anomalies elsewhere in universities. Philosophy especially offers an interesting case study. Like theology, it has changed in its dominant manifestation from being a way of looking at the whole range of reality to a self-definition as one department of knowledge alongside others. For this contraction it too has paid an enormous price, abandoning its historic functions. The university model of the professor of philosophy is one who is well schooled in some portion of the philosophical literature and able to teach it effectively. The ideal publications will be such as to advance the scholarly study of this literature. But the situation is sufficiently porous that some philosophy departments still hire philosophers, that is, persons who think philosophically about a wide range of issues. Similarly, there are occasionally in departments of history persons who address important issues in the current scene from the perspective which their historical research has given them, and, in departments of economics, persons who themselves engage in the constructive task of developing economic theories.

It is my conviction that it is these thinkers, rather than the scholars, who provide what life there still is in the modern university. It is unfortunate, therefore, that the thinker is defined as the anomaly rather than the norm. My suggestion is that a revolution is in order for the sake of the university itself. Instead of attempting to justify ourselves in the context of accepted university ideas, theologians should participate in an offensive against these ideals in favor of thought. The proper ideal of the university would be one that encouraged thinking about the important issues of the day from whatever perspective the several members of the community could bring. In such a university those who thought self-consciously from the Christian perspective would have a fully legitimate role to play.

There is still, however, a feature of theology about which the university is rightly disturbed. Some theologians not only seek truth from the perspective of the Christian faith but also absolutize some features of that faith. That is, they take certain doctrines as beyond criticism or revision, and they affirm their acceptance of those doctrines not on the grounds of their plausibility or illuminating power but on the grounds of sheer authority or irrational decision. One can find analogous habits of mind among philosophers, historians, and economists. Some of them also operate out of fixed convictions which they are not willing to put to the test. But it seems that only theologians have claimed this "dogmatism" as a virtue or even as essential to their perspective.

There is a real question as to how much of this a university can tolerate in its graduate faculty. To exclude it altogether would be to refuse to hear what can be learned from those who at some point challenge the assumptions of the university itself. A healthy institution can include a certain amount of challenge to its own foundations. But the dogmatic spirit is certainly a negative factor in weighing the suitability of anyone for university teaching. Since I find it also antithetical to faith in Christ, I hope that its role in theology will decline. It is, in any case, not that kind of theology whose role in the university I find paradigmatic of what a healthy university should encourage.

A university committed to thought could play a far more positive role in society than do our present universities. Of course, the connection between universities, industry, and government is already very intimate—too intimate for the health of the university. The exploitation of departmental expertise for business and political purposes is not what I have in mind. Rather than expertise, I propose wisdom as the proper concern of the university. The economic order, for example, is far too important to be left to the economists. Historians, sociologists, ecologists, and theologians should address themselves to the economic order with whatever wisdom their diverse perspectives afford them. Of course the church is also far too important to be left to the theologians! Historians, sociologists, ecologists, and economists should address themselves to the church.

It may still be objected that even if a university understood its mission in this way, it should not favor Christianity over other religious traditions by establishing a department of Christian theology. This criticism is far more serious than the others. We are a pluralistic society, and our universities should reflect this pluralism.

It is important, however, to note some irony in the criticism. Most departments of philosophy continue to teach only Western philosophy. English literature has an overwhelmingly favored role in many universities in comparison with other European literatures and even more in comparison with non-European literatures. Why should the major religious tradition of the West not be shown the same favor?

But the fact that departments of philosophy and literature continue to be parochial is not an adequate reason for continuing to be parochial in relation to the great religious traditions. The ideal would be to find a balance in all these areas between the particular importance for us of the traditions that have shaped us and the need to learn from other cultures and traditions as well. Christian theologians should lead the way, precisely for Christian reasons, in calling for a strong voice from other traditions to challenge and enrich our own.

The other tradition that it is most important to represent is Judaism. Judaism shares our Western history with us, and Jews constitute an important minority in most of our universities. In addition, Jews have much to teach Christians about the underside of Christian history, much apart from which our effort to bring our heritage to bear upon current issues is likely to be distorted.

We have learned in this century that there are religious traditions stemming from India and China that are as important as our own when viewed in global perspective both with respect to their power in shaping great civilizations in the past and in their ability to speak convincingly in our own time. The entire university is impoverished if these traditions have no effective expression, and theology suffers most of all.

The question arises whether these other religious traditions must be represented by believing participants or whether a conscientious scholar can present them adequately. The problem is analogous to that in other areas of the university, and certainly the university cannot have advocates for every possible position. In philosophy, for example, a good teacher can present Aristotle and Spinoza adequately even if he or she is neither an Aristotelian nor a Spinozist. The teacher can also do research on these historical figures and contribute to the secondary literature. Similarly, traditional Hindu thought is often very well presented by scholars who are not practicing Hindus. Furthermore, scholars who sympathetically immerse themselves in Hindu literature may be able to contribute to the university's shared quest for wisdom with respect to current problems from a perspective shaped by that immersion.

Nevertheless, there are inherent limitations of scholarship even when it passes over into this kind of wisdom. These can be clarified by contrasting what happens when a skilled historian of religions presents Buddhism and Christianity with deep knowledge and appreciation for both and what happens when a Buddhist and a Christian thinker engage in dialogue. In the former case the two traditions must be taken as already having definite expression. The teacher must present what is to be found in the texts. In the latter case the two traditions are both in the process of change. Students can see Buddhism in the person of a practitioner confronting a new situation and responding to it in an original fashion, and they can see Christianity in the person of a believer being transformed. Neither tradition, insofar as it is alive, can be identified with its texts, and it is insofar as they are both alive that they are of most importance to the student.

Further, if the university wishes to play its role in the whole of society, then by facilitating such dialogue it is making a contribution that accurate and inspired teaching by a disinterested party can never make. The Buddhist and the Christian affected by dialogue alter the condition of the communities in which they live. It is not only student observers who benefit, but also Buddhism and Christianity as living traditions.

II

I have begun with the claim that theology as thinking about important questions from the perspective of Christian faith, instead of being an anomaly in the university, should be a norm. I turn now to a critique of the theological seminary which is hardly less corrupted by the contemporary ideals of the university than is the remainder of the university. Part of its curriculum is justified by subject matter and part by professional training. Both parts are subdivided into departments or specialties, each with its academic guild. One hopes that students, having sampled the fare of this cafeteria of offerings, will be prepared for leadership in the church, but evidence of much success is lacking.

Let me propose that if we set aside the university norms, we could understand ourselves more appropriately. Our task is to prepare leaders for the Christian church. The Christian church is that community which understands itself as constituted by continuity with that history whose center is Jesus Christ. H. Richard Niebuhr helped us to understand what that means when he spoke of the inner history out of which we live. J. B. Metz points in the same direction when he speaks of the importance of our memory. Leaders in the Christian church need to be full participants in this memory, with clear and critical understanding of the history out of which the church lives. They need to be able to bring their Christian identity, formed by this history, to bear on current problems. And they need to be able to help other members of the community to correct, deepen, and broaden their participation in Christian history and also to think as Christians.

This threefold need could organize our seminary curriculum. First there is the study of *our* history through which the understanding of that history is corrected, widened, and deepened. The Bible and the history of the church are the primary elements in that history. This history should be taught, not with neutral objectivity, but as that which constitutes us as what we are. This does not mean that the history is to be presented uncritically. Quite the contrary. Because it tells us who we are both in our strengths and in our weaknesses, it is immensely important that we be accurate. Sentimental views of our past can only get us into trouble.

Second, as we are now constituted by this history, we must deal with the problems and tasks that it bequeathes to us in our contemporary situation. Many of these are baffling. We cannot respond to them by simply recalling how they have been treated in the past. But the richer and more critically accurate are our memories, the more resources we have for fresh and creative response now.

Third, what the entire seminary tries to do for prospective pastors, these pastors must try to do for their people in quite a different setting and with quite different means. The seminary in cooperation with the church must do what it can to equip pastors for this task.

The problems confronted by the church are of many sorts. When we realize what Christian teaching has done in paving the way for the Holocaust, we know that we cannot simply continue to speak as we have spoken. We must reconsider our teaching and our practice.

When we see the confusion among Christian young people about the meaning for them of the sexual revolution and note how little guidance the church offers, we see an important unfilled responsibility.

When we find Christian women struggling for liberation and experiencing the structure, the teaching, and the liturgy of the church opposing them, we are forced to rethink much that we have taken for granted.

When we become aware that some patterns of church government operate in opposition to Christian teaching about human relations, we see that the day-by-day activities of the parish need to be considered again in the light of our Christian memories.

The departmental or disciplinary structure of seminaries works against the serious consideration of these and scores of other important questions. They do not fall neatly in any discipline. They involve theology, ethics, sociology of religion, Christian education, preaching, liturgics, pastoral counseling, and other disciplines as well. Indeed, few of the real issues faced by Christians as individuals or as the church fall conveniently into our disciplines. It is time to concern ourselves much more with the real problems and much less with our academic disciplines.

Consider my own discipline of systematic theology. Are any of the above appropriate topics for me to consider? The question is serious; but can one imagine an Augustine, or a Luther, or even a Tillich asking such a question? Surely not. They did not need to, because their identity was not bound up with a discipline. Once systematic theology becomes a discipline alongside others, then the question does arise. In order to answer it I must devote myself to defining the discipline, its subject matter, its methods, and its interconnections with other disciplines. Such questions can keep me occupied. Dealing with them can even give me the illusion that I am doing something important rather than simply inventing and solving unnecessary and artificial problems. I am not likely to get around to considering the real issues facing the church.

On the other hand, if to be a theologian is nothing other than to be one who thinks about important questions self-consciously as a Christian, then I will not try first to work out my subject matter and methods but will try to understand the problems and see what I can do to respond appropriately to them. Of course I will need help from those who know more about various facets of the issues. But I will not draw a line between theory and practice, turning over to others the task of developing the practical implications. If I see that changes are needed in other fields, I will not hesitate to express my views. For example, as part of the Christian response to the Holocaust, I will suggest that in the future the history we teach as *our* history include the story of the Jews from the time of Jesus to the present. But I will not be troubled if others also deal with some of the same problems I have selected, bringing to them their different experience and skills.

My concern is that all of us who try to throw light on the issues of our day, whether they are the specific tasks of professional ministry or global crises, understand ourselves as theologians, that is, as Christians who think self-consciously as Christians. There is no harm in some of us concentrating on how to deal with problems in the personal lives of parishioners and others on world hunger. There is no harm either in some of us concentrating on the problems caused by the lack of fit between the contemporary world view and traditional formulations of what Christians believe. There is no harm in some of us being better versed in psychology, others in sociology, and still others in philosophy. Indeed, these diversities can enrich our life together and our ability collectively to serve the church. But there is harm in our erecting departmental barriers that divide us and in our seeking to give our reflection within our departments the dignity of a discipline. We have suffered much from that; our students have suffered more; and the church may have suffered most of all.

The most urgent problem for the church today is that of attaining a shared clarity about its mission. Like Emory University, I am a part of the United Methodist denomination. Our denomination from the beginning was organized for the sake of mission. Today much of the organization remains, but there is no effective consensus as to the mission it should serve. As a result, the structures once designed to enable local congregations to participate in the mission of the whole church are now directed to assisting the local parish in its internal life. We who live with the memory of Jesus' saying that those who try to save their lives will lose them know that this is decadence. We cannot be saved from this decadence by moral condemnation or seeking someone to blame. We can only be saved by hearing God's call.

I have no doubt that God is calling. The needs of the world have never been more urgent. The resources directed to meeting those needs are few and becoming scarcer. The survival of the human race itself may well be at stake. It is strange that in all this the church finds nothing that calls it to heroic action comparable to that of earlier generations. But this strange situation obtains not only in our denomination but in most of the others. We are all becoming more ingrown and defensive. We seem to have no organ with which to listen to God's call. For listening is hard and disciplined work that takes time and effort and needs to be done in community. The Council of Bishops cannot do this. General Conference cannot do this. The boards and agencies are established to carry out the mandates of the church, not to think. That leaves the seminaries.

As we are presently structured, we too are incapable of listening to God's call to the church. We each have our own disciplines to attend to and our academic peers to impress. The church looks to us for scattered expertise, not for wisdom. Nevertheless, as communities of Christian thinkers we have the opportunity to speak with wisdom and to point out alternatives to continued decline.

We need to do this both for the sake of the church as a whole and, more immediately, in order to discharge our responsibility to our students. There can be no more important topic of Christian reflection for our students or for ourselves than the church and the ministry of its ordained leadership in the light of the mission to which it is called. This can be called pastoral theology, but when pastoral theology is developed apart from the global mission of the church, it is in danger of encouraging the inward turning which is our decadence. On the other hand, pastoral theology in the light of the inclusive Christian mission is a unifying topic to which the entire faculty should contribute.

But even this does not exhaust the task. God's concern finally is for the world rather than only for the church in its mission to the world. Christians, including pastors, need to think about many things, some very abstract, some very immediate and particular, as Christians. This larger task subsumes pastoral theology without shifting from its practical bent. Although practical theology has often been identified with pastoral theology, and even with a pastoral theology insensitive to the mission of the church to the world, there is today a move to use the term in a much broader sense. In this most inclusive sense, practical theology is the center of the theological curriculum. It is made possible by the formation of Christian identity through historical study and it determines what roles pastors are to play and the skills they need to acquire.

III

The occasion for the series of which this essay is a part is the discussion in the graduate program at Emory of a track for the study of constructive theology. My comments to date have dealt with the place of such study in the university and the nature of education for ministry. I assume that if the program is to succeed, constructive theology must be accepted as appropriate to the university and that the reason for concern for constructive theology is the need of the

church and its seminaries. However, I want to make a few statements more directly on the subject of my understanding of the
enterprise of constructive theology.

Constructive theology is, so far as I can tell, a uniquely Christian
enterprise. It depends upon a radically historical understanding of
a tradition. Such an understanding indicates that no past formulation
of faith can suffice for the present, just as all present formulations
will prove inadequate for the future. It militates against all absolutist
claims.

There remains a tendency among Christian thinkers to resist the
wholly historical and therefore relative understanding of our task.
Many think of themselves as distinguishing the unchanging essense
of Christianity from its historically conditioned garments. But this
will not do. The definition of the essence proves to be just as historically conditioned as any other feature of theology.

Others recognize that there can be no unchanging essence but
suppose that at least there are unchanging topics that constitute the
perennial task of constructive theology. There is more justification
for this view. However, it, too, ultimately limits rather than supports
constructive theology. Topics that are important in one century
move to the sidelines in another. New topics arise. Today the meaning of the possible, even probable, end of the life of the human
species through our own foolishness is theologically crucial for Christians. It can, of course, be understood as falling under the traditional
topic of eschatology. But the truth is that our sense of this likely
end is too different from the traditional doctrine of the end for the
suggestion to be helpful that it is the same topic. As a matter of
fact, theologians seeking to restrict themselves to the traditional
topics of Christianity have simply not faced the actual situation in
which we find ourselves. From one point of view it is astonishing
that theologians of hope, of the future, and of liberation ignore the
threatening catastrophe. But when we see how strong is the impetus
to deal only with traditional topics, even if in new ways, we can
understand that the self-destruction of the human race falls outside
such theology. We can understand, but we cannot condone. We
must not define constructive theology simply as the deconstruction
and reconstruction of traditional doctrines or the further refinement

of traditional topics. Constructive theology should be instead responsible Christian thinking about those matters which seem most important to us.

I do not believe that reflection about the most important questions facing us today will lead to discontinuity with our Christian past. Indeed, it is likely to uncover deeper continuities than is the direct effort to treat the same problems. Those problems, in the ages when theology was taken seriously, were the ones that seemed most important. Continuing to deal with them when they no longer seem so urgent actually breaks the continuity. To wrestle with one's whole being with the deepest issues of our time will renew that continuity. Nothing less is worthy of the task of constructive theology.

IV

I was invited to share in this colloquium in part as a representative of process theology. In conclusion I should perhaps say something about what it means to be a process theologian and in what sense what I have been saying thus far is an expression of process theology.

First, it is important to remind you that process theology is an unstructured movement. There has never been a meeting at which a party line was adopted. Some who are designated by this label would not approve my ideas. I speak only for myself.

Further, I would be disappointed if my proposals could be convincing only to those who shared my commitment to a particular philosophy. In that case they would have no chance of implementation at all. My claim for the process perspective is that it enables me to see some things that need to be pointed out. If when they are pointed out, others agree that they are worthy of note, then some consensus may gradually emerge. If they do not appear important when viewed from other perspectives, then I need to understand and engage those perspectives more seriously and also to question my judgments.

Nevertheless, I will try to show how my proposals do grow out of the hold of the process perspective upon me. I can trace three lines of thought of which I am conscious.

First, if all is in process, this is certainly true for thinking. I cannot nail down a fixed starting point on the basis of which to construct a system. The process of trying to nail that down places me in a different position from the one I was in before. To bind myself to the place I was when I first began nailing is to refuse the new life and possibilities God gives me now. To think freely is to think where I am now and as all my experience leads me to think now. That is, I am constituted by the whole of the past and now deal with the new situation as so constituted. Insofar as I am constituted as a Christian, I think as a Christian, and that thinking is part of my future constitution as a Christian.

I certainly do not oppose systematic thinking. I oppose only the effort to stabilize thought at the point of that system. When I really think systematically about some problem, I find that this activity alters me in such a way that I immediately face different questions and new problems. It does not make sense to me to teach students a system from which they can then minister. It does make sense to encourage them to think seriously as Christians about the real problems of the church. In doing so, there will certainly be systematic elements in the way they think.

As I have experienced the process of intellectual change, it has not been primarily reversal of previous opinions. The process is chiefly one of expansion, although that expansion relativizes and alters much that was thought from a more limited perspective. I feel little need to disown what I wrote twenty years ago, but I would not write it today.

Second, in the past few years I have come to contrast the ecological model of things with the substantial one that has been dominant for centuries. I learned the ecological model, chiefly from Whitehead, although I now formulate it in my own way. The ecological model, under various names, seems to be gaining ground, and I rejoice in that. This is a model of interconnectedness, of internal relations. According to the ecological model, nothing is what it is in itself; everything is constituted by its relations to other things.

I have come to realize how very deeply we have all been governed by the notion of real things as separated from one another with fixed boundaries and capable of existing independently. These are the atoms of Greek philosophy and modern science. Their substantial autonomy allows us to separate them from one another and thus to investigate them and the objects that are composed of them. With this understanding we could develop separate disciplines to study separate segments of reality without falsifying what we studied.

But if, as I am convinced, this substantialist model of the physical world is false, then the structures of thought that have been developed on this model are also false. Above all, the division of knowledge into separate compartments is inappropriate. Further, it is dangerous. Many of our bodily ills cannot be healed when we are approached compartmentally. Holistic medicine has proved its worth. An economics not informed by ecology speeds us on the way to catastrophe. Military policy not affected by a humanistic and sociological understanding of the peoples we would subdue does not work. The church and ministry are falsified when they are approached in isolated segments.

It has taken me a long time to apply this ecological perspective to theological education. It is more comfortable to look farther away. I really do not want to upset my colleagues. We have just voted a new curriculum, and I have no desire to go through the process of curricular reform again soon. But from where I have now come I seem to see that theological schools are blocked and blinded by their departmental structure and that until we give up our illusions of autonomous disciplines, we cannot serve the urgent needs of the church.

In the third place, my belief that in dialogue with Buddhists, Christianity can be transformed without ceasing to be Christianity also expresses what I have learned from Whitehead. He has taught me that every moment of my experience not only inherits from my personal past but also is influenced by many other events. The question is what I do with those multiple influences. To simplify and illustrate, consider the case in which I hear a new idea that is in apparent contradiction to what I have thought. What happens? I can simply reject it. I can accept it in place of my previous opinion. I can work out a compromise that omits much of what is of value in both ideas. But it is also possible that I can come to a new position which holds both of the ideas in a contrast, allowing each to contribute its distinctive truth. This is the way in which real growth takes place. Whitehead shows that this growth can occur only because of the effective working of God in my experience. It is grace.

The new position to which I come is truly different from the one at which I was before. But it is not discontinuous. The old position is still there, only it is transformed.

The microscopic model of individual human experiences illumines for me also what takes place historically in the meeting of two traditions. Indeed, finally, what happens historically can in principle be analyzed into what happens in individual human experiences. I believe that my own thinking has been creatively transformed in my encounter with Buddhism, and I hope for further transformation. I do not believe I have become less Christian in the process. What happens in me happens also in other Christians in diverse ways in this historic meeting of Christians and Buddhists. I look at the transformation of Christianity in its encounter with the East as not less important than its earlier transformation through Hellenism.

Again I would stress that the insights to which I have been brought through process thought are not a monopoly of process theologians. Similar insights can come to those shaped by other theological traditions. And it is possible to appropriate insights attained through one history of thought within another without appropriating the whole structure within which it arose.

In view of this, one may ask, Why be a process theologian? The answer from the perspective of process theology is: Don't be, unless it is helpful and illuminating. If Tillich or Barth throws more light upon the important issues that the church faces in today's world, then follow them. Thus far I have found that I can assimilate what I learn from them within a Whiteheadian context, whereas there are features of Whitehead's thought, important to me, that are not readily assimilable within a Tillichian or a Barthian framework. That is why I am a process theologian.

8

Theology as
the Expression of
God's Liberating Activity
for the Poor

JAMES H. CONE

Theology is language about God. *Christian* theology is language about God's liberating activity in the world on behalf of the freedom of the oppressed.[1] Any talk about God that fails to make God's liberation of the oppressed its starting point is not Christian. It may be philosophical and have some relation to Scripture, but it is not Christian. For the word "Christian" connects theology inseparably to God's will to set the captives free.[2]

I realize that this understanding of theology and Christianity is not the central view of the Western theological tradition, nor is it the dominant viewpoint of contemporary Euro-American theology. However, truth ought not to be defined by the majority or by the dominant intellectual interest of university academicians. The purpose of this essay is to examine the theological presuppositions that underlie the claim that Christian theology is language about God's liberation of the victim from social and political oppression.

1. My contention that Christian theology is language about God's liberating activity for the poor is based on the assumption that the Scripture is the primary source of theological speech.[3] To use Scripture as the starting point of theology does not rule out other sources, such as philosophy, tradition, and our contemporary context. It simply means that the Scripture will define how these sources will function in theology.

That Christian theology must begin with Scripture appears self-evident. Without this basic witness, Christianity would be meaningless. This point seems so obvious to me that it is almost impossible to think otherwise. However, the point does need clarification. There are many perspectives on Scripture. There are some who regard it as infallible, and there are others who say that it is simply an important body of literature. There are nearly as many perspectives on Scripture as there are theologians. While I cannot assess the validity of the major viewpoints, I can state what I believe to be the central message of Scripture.[4]

I believe that my perspective on Scripture is derived from Scripture itself. Since others, with different perspectives, would say the same thing, I can only explain the essential structure of my hermeneutical perspective. It seems clear to me that whatever else we may say about Scripture, it is first and foremost a story of Israelite people who believed that Yahweh was involved in their history. In the Old Testament, the story begins with the first exodus of Hebrew slaves from Egypt and continues through the second exodus from Babylon and the rebuilding of the Temple. To be sure, there are many ways of looking at this story, but the import of the biblical message is clear on this point: God's salvation is revealed in the liberation of slaves from sociopolitical bondage. Indeed, God's judgment is inflicted on the people of Israel when they humiliate the poor and the orphans. "You shall not ill-treat any widow or fatherless child. If you do, be sure that I will listen if they appeal to me; my anger will be roused and I will kill you with the sword" (Exod. 22:23–24, NEB). Of course, there are other themes in the Old Testament, and they are important. But their importance is found in their illumination of the central theme of divine liberation. To fail to see this point is to misunderstand the Old Testament and thus to distort its message.

My contention that the Scripture is the story of God's liberation of the poor also applies to the New Testament, where the story is carried to universal dimensions. The New Testament does not invalidate the Old. The meaning of Jesus Christ is found in God's will to make liberation not simply the property of one people but of all of humankind. God became a poor Jew in Jesus and thus identified with the helpless in Israel. The cross of Jesus is nothing but God's will to be with and like the poor. The resurrection means that God achieved victory over oppression, so that the poor no longer have to be determined by their poverty. This is true not only for "the house of Israel" but for all the wretched of the land. The incarnation, then, is simply God taking upon the divine self human suffering and humiliation. The resurrection is the divine victory over suffering, the bestowal of freedom to all who are weak and helpless. This and nothing else is the central meaning of the biblical story.

If theology is derived from this divine story, then it must be a language about liberation. Anything else would be an ideological distortion of the gospel message.

2. Because Christian theology begins and ends with the biblical story of God's liberation of the weak, it is also christological language.[5] On this point Karl Barth was right. Unfortunately Barth did not explicate this christological point with sufficient clarity, because his theology was determined too much by the theological tradition of Augustine and Calvin and too little by Scripture. While Barth's christological starting point enabled him to move closer to the biblical message than most of his contemporaries, his understanding of theology was not derived from the biblical view of Jesus Christ as the liberator of the oppressed. Because Jesus the liberator is not central in Barth's Christology, his view of theology is also defective at this point.

Because theology begins with Scripture, it must also begin with Christ. Christian theology is language about the crucified and risen Christ who grants freedom to all who are falsely condemned in an oppressive society. What else can the crucifixion mean except that God, the Holy One of Israel, became identified with the victims of oppression? What else can the resurrection mean except that God's victory in Christ is the poor person's victory over poverty? If theology does not take this seriously, how can it be worthy of the name Christian? If the church, the community out of which theology arises, does not make God's liberation of the oppressed central in its mission and proclamation, how can it rest easy, with a condemned criminal as the dominant symbol of its message?

3. Because Christian theology is more than the retelling of the biblical story, it also must do more than exegete Scripture. The meaning of the Scripture is not self-evident in every situation. Therefore it is theology's task to relate the message of the Bible to every situation. This is not an easy task, since situations are different, and God's word to humanity is not always self-evident.[6]

Because theology must relate the message to the situation of the church's involvement in the world, theology must use other sources in addition to Scripture. On this point, Bultmann and Tillich are more useful than Barth, although they misrepresented the function of culture in theology. My disagreement with Bultmann and Tillich, unlike with Barth, is not on whether theology should use culture (for example, philosophy, sociology, and psychology) in the interpretation of the gospel. That our language about God is inseparably bound with our own historicity seems so obvious that to deny it is to become enslaved to our own ideology.[7] Karl Barth notwithstanding, the natural theology issue is dead, at least to the extent that our language is never simply about God and nothing else, however much we might wish it otherwise. This means that theology cannot avoid philosophy and other perspectives on the world.

The issue, then, is not whether we can or ought to avoid speaking of human culture in the doing of theology. Rather, the question is whether divine revelation in Scripture grants us a possibility of saying something about God that is not simply about ourselves. Unless this possibility is given, however small it might be, there seems to be no point in talking about the distinction between white and black theology or the difference between falsehood and truth.

I believe that by focusing on the Scripture, theology is granted the freedom to take seriously its social and political situation without being determined by it. Thus the question is not whether we take seriously our social existence, but *how* and in *what* way we take it seriously. Whose social situation does our theology represent? For whom do we speak? The importance of the Scripture in our theology is that it can help us to answer that question so as to represent the political interest of the One about whom Christianity speaks. By using Scripture, we are forced by Scripture itself to focus on our social existence, but not merely in terms of our own interests, though that is always involved. Scripture can liberate theology to be Christian in the contemporary situation. It can break the theologians out of their social ideologies and enable them to hear a word that is other than their own consciousness.

This "other" in theology is distinct but never separated from our social existence. God became human in Christ, so that we are free to speak about God in terms of humanity. Indeed, any other talk is not about the crucified and risen Lord. The presence of the crucified and risen Lord as witnessed in Scripture determines whose social interest we must represent if we are to be faithful to him.

In an attempt to do theology in the light of this scriptural witness to the crucified and risen Christ as he is found in our contemporary situation, I have spoken of Christian theology as black theology.[8] Of course there are other ways of talking about God which are also Christian. I have never denied that, and do not wish to deny it now. Christian theology can be written from the perspective of red, brown, and yellow peoples. It can also be written in the light of feminine experience. In Japan, I have been impressed by the way Korean Christians are hearing the word of divine liberation in an oppressive Japanese culture. Christian theology can also be written from the perspective of class, as has been profoundly disclosed in the writings of Latin American liberation theologians. It is also possible to combine the issues of class, sex, and color, as was recently attempted in Letty Russell's book *Human Liberation in a Feminist Perspective*. The possibilities are many and varied. There is not one Christian theology, but many Christian theologies which are valid expressions of the gospel of Jesus.

But what is not possible is to do Christian theology apart from the biblical claim that God came in Christ to set the captives free.[9] It is not possible to do Christian theology as if the poor do not exist. Indeed, there can be no Christian speech about God which does not represent the interest of the victims in our society. If we could just make that point an embodiment of our Christian identity, then we will have moved a long way since the days of Constantine.

4. Because Christian theology is language about God's liberation of the weak as defined by the Scripture in relation to our contemporary situation, Christian theology is inseparably connected with an oppressed community. If God is the God of the poor who is liberating from bondage, how else can we speak correctly about this God unless our language arises out of the community where God's presence is found? If Christian theology is language about the crucified and risen One, the One who has elected all for freedom, what else can it be other than the language of those who are fighting for freedom?

My limitation of Christian theology to the oppressed community does not mean that everything the oppressed say about God is right because they are weak and helpless. To do that would be to equate the oppressed's word with God's Word. There is nothing in the Scripture that grants this possibility. When the oppressed are inclined to use their position as a privilege, as an immunity from error, they do well to remember the Scripture's witness to God's righteousness as other than anything human. On this point, Karl Barth was right: there is an infinite qualitative distinction between God and humanity.

When I limit Christian theology to the oppressed community, I intend to say nothing other than what I believe to be the central message of the Scripture: God has chosen to disclose divine righteousness in the liberation of the poor. Therefore to be outside of this community is to be in a place where one is excluded from the possibility of hearing and obeying God's Word of liberation. By becoming poor and entrusting divine revelation to a carpenter from Nazareth, God makes clear where one has to be in order to hear the divine Word and experience divine presence. If Jesus had been born in the king's court and had been an adviser to the emperor of Rome, then what I am saying would have no validity. If Jesus had made no distinction between the rich and the poor, the weak and the strong, then the Christian gospel would not be a word of liberation to the oppressed. If Jesus had not been crucified as a criminal of Rome and condemned as a blasphemer by the Jewish religious leaders, then my claim about Christian theology and the oppressed would be meaningless. It is because the Scripture is so decisively clear on this issue that I insist that theology cannot separate itself from the cultural history of the oppressed if it intends to be faithful to the One who makes Christian language possible.

What, then, are we to say about these other so-called Christian theologies? To the extent that they fail to remain faithful to the central message of the gospel, they are heretical.[10] In saying this, I do not intend to suggest that I have the whole truth and nothing but the truth. In fact, I could be the heretic. Furthermore, I do not believe that the purpose of identifying heresy is to be able to identify the "good" people from the "bad" or infallible truth from error. I merely intend to say what I believe to be faithful to the gospel of Jesus as witnessed in the Scripture, nothing more and nothing less. If we do not say what we believe, in love and faith and the hope that we are speaking and doing the truth, then why speak at all? If there is no distinction between truth and error, the gospel and heresy, then there is no way to say what Christian theology is. We must be able to say when language is not Christian, if not always at least sometimes.

I must say that white North American theology is heresy not because I want to burn anybody at the stake. Far too many of my people have been lynched for me to suggest such nonsense. The identification of heresy is not for the purpose of making ultimate decisions about who shall live or die and who will be saved or damned. To know what heresy is, is to know what appears to be truth but is actually untruth. Thus it is for the sake of the truth of the gospel that we must say what truth is not.

The saying of what truth is, is intimately connected with the doing of truth. To know the truth is to do the truth. Speaking and doing are bound together, so that what we say can be authenticated only by what we do. Unfortunately, the Western church has not always been clear on this point. Its mistake has often been the identification of heresy with word rather than action. By failing to explicate the connection between word and action, the church tended to identify the gospel with right speech and thus became the chief heretic. The church became so preoccupied with its own spoken word about God that it failed to hear and thus live according to God's word of freedom for the poor. From Augustine to Schleiermacher, it is hard to find a theologian in the Western church who defines the gospel in terms of God's liberation of the oppressed.

The same is true in much of the contemporary speech about God. It can be seen in the separation of theology from ethics and the absence of liberation in both. The chief mistake of contemporary theology is not simply found in what it says about God, though that is not excluded. It is found in its separation of theory from praxis, and the absence of liberation in its analysis of the gospel.

5. The limitation of Christian theology to the oppressed community not only helps us to identify heresy, it also helps us to reexamine the sources of theological speech. The language of liberation must reflect the experiences of the people about whom we claim to speak. To say that one's speech is a theology of liberation

does not in itself mean that it represents the oppressed. There are many theologies of liberation, not all of which represent the weak and the helpless. The difference between liberation theology in general and liberation theology in the Christian perspective is found in whether the language about freedom is derived from one's participation in the oppressed people's struggle. If one's language about freedom is derived from one's involvement in oppressed people's struggle for freedom, then it is Christian language. It is a language that is accountable to the God encountered in the oppressed community, not to some abstract God in a theological textbook. To say that one's theology represents the poor means that the representation reflects the words and deeds of the poor. The theologian begins to talk like the poor, to pray like the poor, and to preach with the poor in mind. Instead of making Barth, Tillich, and Pannenberg the exclusive sources for the doing of theology,[11] the true liberation theologian is compelled to hear the cries and the moans of the people who sing, "I wish I knew how it would feel to be free, I wish I could break all the chains holdin' me."

What would theology look like if we were to take seriously the claim that Christian theology is poor people's speech about their hopes and dreams that one day "trouble will be no more"? One thing is certain: it would not look like most of the papers presented in the American Academy of Religion and the American Theological Society. Neither would it look like "process theology," "liberal theology," "Death of God theology," and a host of other adjectives that academicians use to describe their intellectual endeavors.

Theology derived from the moans and shouts of oppressed black people defines a different set of problems than those found in the white theological textbooks. Instead of asking whether the Bible is infallible, black people want to know whether it is real, that is, whether the God to whom it bears witness is present in their struggle. Black theology seeks to investigate the meaning of black people's confidence in the biblical claim that Jesus is the way, the truth, and the life. Black theology is the consciousness of the people analyzing the meaning of their faith when they have to live in an extreme situation of suffering. How can black theology remain faithful to the people and the God revealed in their struggle if it does not respect the people's conceptualizations of their claim that "God will make a way of no way"? They really believe that

> When you are troubled, burdened with care,
> And know not what to do;
> Fear ye not to call his Name
> And he will fix it for you.

Theology derived from the black experience must reflect the rhythm and the mood, the passion and the ecstasy, the joy and the sorrow of a people in struggle to free themselves from the shackles of oppression. This theology must be black because the people are black. It must deal with liberation because the people are oppressed. It must be biblical because the people claim that the God of the exodus and the prophets and of Jesus and the apostle Paul is involved in their history, liberating them from bondage. A theology derived from black sources would have to focus on Jesus Christ as the beginning and the end of faith, because this affirmation is a summary of the black testimony that "Jesus picked me up, turned me round, left my feet on solid ground." He is sometimes called the "Wheel in the middle of the Wheel," the "Rose of Sharon," and the "Lord of Life." Black people claim that he healed the sick, gave sight to the blind, and enabled the lame to walk. "Jesus," they said, "do most anything."

6. The presence of Jesus as the starting point of black theology does not mean that it can overlook the experience of suffering in black life.[12] Any theology that takes liberation seriously must also take seriously the continued presence of suffering in black life. How can we claim that "God will fix it" for the poor when the poor still exist in poverty? The blues, folklore, and other secular expressions are constant reminders that a simplistic view of divine liberation is never adequate for a people in struggle against oppression. Black religion has never been silent on the theme of suffering. Indeed, black faith arose out of black people's experience of suffering. Without the brokenness of black existence, its pain and sorrow, there would be no reason for the existence of black faith.

> Nobody knows the trouble I've seen,
> Nobody knows my sorrow,
> Nobody knows the trouble I've seen,
> Glory Hallelujah!

The "Glory Hallelujah" at the end of that spiritual was not a denial of trouble but a faith affirmation that trouble does not have the last word on black existence. It means that evil and suffering, while still unquestionably present, cannot count decisively against black people's faith that Jesus is also present with them, fighting against trouble. His divine presence counts more than the pain that the people experience in their history. Jesus is the people's "rock in a weary land" and their "shelter in a time of storm." No matter how difficult the pains of life might become, they cannot destroy the people's confidence that victory over suffering has already been won in Jesus' resurrection. Thus the people sang:

> Sometimes I hangs my head an' cries,
> But Jesus goin' to wipe my weep'n eyes.

Of course, there is no evidence that black people's faith claim is "objectively" or "scientifically" true. Thus when William Jones, a black critic of black North American theology, asks about the decisive liberation event in black history, he is asking the question from a vantage point that is external to black faith.[13] For black faith claims that Jesus is the only evidence one needs to have in order to be assured that God has not left the little ones alone in bondage. For those who stand outside this faith, such a claim is a scandal, that is, foolishness to those whose wisdom is derived from European intellectual history. "But to those who are called, . . . Christ [is] the power of God and the wisdom of God" (1 Cor. 1:24). In black religion, Christ is the Alpha and the Omega, the One who has come to make the first last and the last first. The knowledge of truth is not found in philosophy, sociology, or psychology. It is found in the immediate presence of Jesus with the people, "buildin' them up where they are torn down and proppin' them up on every leanin' side." The evidence that Jesus is liberating them from bondage is found in their walking and talking with him, telling him all about their troubles. It is found in the courage and strength he bestows on the people as they struggle to humanize their environment.

These answers may not satisfy the problem of theodicy as defined by Sartre and Camus. But black faith assertions were never intended to be answers for the intellectual problems arising out of the European experience. They are *black* reflections on life and were intended as testimonies for the oppressed so that they would not give up in despair. They are not rational arguments. Thus the truth of the claims is not found in whether the black faith perspective answers the theodicy problems as posed in Camus's *Plague* or Sartre's *Being and Nothingness*.[14] The truth of the black faith claim is found in whether the people receive that extra strength to fight until freedom comes. Its truth is found in whether the people who are the victims of white philosophy and theology are led to struggle to realize the freedom they talk about. The same is true for a black theology or philosophy that seeks to speak on behalf of the people. Whether William Jones is right or whether my analysis is correct should not be decided on theoretical criteria derived from Western theology and philosophy. Pure theory is for those who have the leisure for reflection but not for the victims of the land. The truth, therefore, of our theological analysis ought to be decided by the historical function of our assertions in the community we claim to represent. Whose analysis, Cone's or Jones's, leads to the historical praxis against oppression? I would contend that black humanism, as derived from Camus and Sartre, does not lead the people to the fight against oppression but rather to give up in despair, the feeling that there is little I can do about white power. But my analysis of black faith, with Jesus as the "Captain of the Old Ship of Zion," can lead the people to believe that their fight is not in vain. That was why Martin Luther King, Jr., could move the people to fight for justice. He had a dream that was connected with Jesus. Without Jesus, the people would have remained passive, and content with humiliation and suffering. When I turn to Western philosophy's analysis of metaphysics and ontology, I do not know whether King was right, if rightness is defined by white rationality. But in the faith context of black religion, King was right, because people were led to act out the faith they talked about. If black theology is to be a theology of and for this black faith, it will not bother too much about the logical contradictions of its assertions when they are compared with white Western philosophy. William Jones's humanism notwithstanding, some of us black folk still believe that

> Without God I could do nothing;
> Without God my life would fail;
> Without God my life would be rugged,
> Just like a ship without a sail.

Note the absence of philosophical skepticism in the next stanza:

> Without a doubt, he is my Savior,
> Yes my strength along my way;
> Yes in deep water, he is my anchor,
> And through faith he'll keep me all the way.

It is because black people feel secure in "leaning and depending on Jesus" that they often lift their voices in praise and adoration, singing: "Thank you, Jesus, I thank you, Lord. For you brought me a mighty long ways. You've been my doctor, you've been my lawyer, and you've been my friend. You've been my everything!" The people actually believe that with Jesus' presence, they cannot lose. Victory over suffering and oppression is certain. If not now, then in God's own "good time" "one day, it will all be over." We will "cross the river of Jordan" and "sit down with the Father and argue with the Son" and "tell them about the world we just come from." Thus, black people's struggle of freedom is not in vain. This is what black people mean when they sing, "I'm so glad that trouble don't last always." Because trouble does not have the last word, we can fight *now* in order to realize in our present what we know to be coming in God's future.

NOTES

1. The identification of the Christian gospel with the liberation of the oppressed and of Christian theology with the explication of the meaning of the struggle of freedom is the essence of black theology. The term "black theology" was first used in this connection with the publication of my book *Black Theology and Black Power* (New York: Seabury Press, 1969), 117. "The task of Black Theology . . . is to analyze the black man's condition in the light of God's revelation in Jesus Christ with the purpose of creating a new understanding of black dignity among black people, and providing the necessary soul in that people, to destroy white racism" (p. 117). This definition of theology connects it with reflection and praxis and the struggle of the oppressed.

The second published book on black theology was my *A Black Theology of Liberation* (Philadelphia: J. B. Lippincott Co., 1970). Here the theme of liberation is made the organizing principle of a systematic theology and it is the very first one to do so. (Gustavo Gutiérrez's *A Theology of Liberation* was published in 1971.) "Christian theology is a theology of liberation. It is a rational study of the being of God in the world in the light of the existential situation of an oppressed community, relating the forces of liberation to the essence of the gospel which is Jesus Christ" (p. 17).

These two books represent the beginning of black theology and its identification of the gospel with liberation. However, while the term "black
theology" does not appear on the theological scene until the publication of
my book in 1969, the relating of the gospel with the struggle of freedom
is an integral part of the black religious tradition from the time of slavery
to the present. See my books *The Spirituals and the Blues* (New York:
Seabury Press, 1972) and *Black Theology and Black Power*, chap. 4; also
Gayraud S. Wilmore, *Black Religion and Black Radicalism* (New York:
Doubleday & Co., 1972).

2. For a much deeper explication of my theological presuppositions on
this point, see, in addition to my above-mentioned books, my *God of the
Oppressed* (New York: Seabury Press, 1975).

3. See especially *A Black Theology of Liberation*, chap. 2, "The Sources
and Norm of Black Theology," and *God of the Oppressed*, chaps. 2 and 4.

4. See especially *God of the Oppressed*, chap. 4, "Biblical Revelation
and Social Existence."

5. For the clearest explication of this point on Christology and its relation
to theology, see *God of the Oppressed*, chap. 6, "Who Is Jesus Christ for
Us Today?" See also *A Black Theology of Liberation*, chap. 6, "Christ in
Black Theology"; *Black Theology and Black Power*, chap. 2, "The Gospel
of Jesus, Black People, and Black Power"; and *The Spirituals and the Blues*,
chap. 3, "God and Jesus Christ in the Black Spirituals."

The christological center and biblical source of my theology is perhaps
the most debated theme among black theologians. Many black theologians
think that it is too narrow and excludes too many religious dimensions in
the black community, especially the so-called "secular." Others have at-
tributed the christological focus of my theology to a certain Barthian de-
pendence. I do not agree with these critiques. For a discussion of this
debate, see Wilmore, *Black Religion and Black Radicalism*, 298ff. For my
response to Wilmore, see my *God of the Oppressed*, chap. 2, n. 38, pp.
252f.

6. The complexity of this hermeneutical task is the primary concern of
my *God of the Oppressed*.

7. For a detailed discussion of the problem of ideology, see *God of the
Oppressed*, chap. 2, "The Social Context of Theology," and chap. 4, "Black
Theology and Ideology." See also my article "Schwarze Theologie und
Ideologie: Eine Antwort an meine Gesprachspartner," *Evangelische Theologie*, January/February 1974 (Munich: Chr. Kaiser Verlag); the same article
also appears in English in *Union Seminary Quarterly Review* 31, no. 1 (Fall
1975).

8. My theology has often been characterized as too exclusive by white
European theologians, but it is only exclusive in its limitation of the gospel
with the liberation of the victims and not at the point of skin color. In my
first book, *Black Theology and Black Power*, I wrote, "Being reconciled to

God does not mean that one's skin is physically black. It essentially depends on the color of your heart, soul, and mind" (p. 151). In *A Black Theology of Liberation,* I wrote: "The focus on blackness does not mean that only blacks suffer as victims in a racist society, but that blackness is an ontological symbol and a visible reality which best describes what oppression means in America. The extermination of Indians, the persecution of Jews, the oppression of Mexican Americans, and every other conceivable inhumanity done in the name of God and country—these brutalities can be analyzed in terms of America's inability to recognize humanity in persons of color" (pp. 27–28). This is enough evidence to show that I never naively thought that black people were the only victims. Liberation theology must take seriously oppression in any form. However, we must not universalize oppression so that its distinctive character and form in a specific setting is lost. This is what happens when the rulers and those who represent them co-opt the language of oppression and liberation. I think this is happening in the popularity of liberation theology among Euro-American white rulers and theologians. For a deeper discussion of the oppression of the oppressor, see *God of the Oppressed,* chap. 7, "The Meaning of Liberation," especially 146f.

9. I have developed this point in many places: See especially *God of the Oppressed,* 81f. Everything I have written has been an explication of this central thesis.

10. For an additional discussion of heresy in the context of the history of the Christian tradition and the theological task, see *God of the Oppressed,* 36f. See also *Black Theology and Black Power,* chap. 3, "The White Church and Black Power."

11. Much of this tendency in theology is being corrected with the development of liberation theology in Latin America, political theology in Europe and North America, women's liberation theology in North America, the theology of hope and black theology in North America and South Africa. But I still think we have a long way to go on this issue. We need to take theology out of the classroom and let it happen in the community of the oppressed in their struggle of freedom. Otherwise all our talk about liberation theology will be just that: talk and nothing else. Such a theology serves only the rulers. That is why again I think that Christian theology is limited to an oppressed community.

12. For a further discussion of the theme of suffering in black religion, see *The Spirituals and the Blues,* chap. 4, "God and Black Suffering"; see also *God of the Oppressed,* chap. 8, "Divine Liberation and Black Suffering." This theme has been much discussed by other black writers. See especially William Jones, *Is God a White Racist?* (New York: Doubleday & Co., 1973).

13. See Jones's *Is God a White Racist?*; for a fuller critique of Jones, see my *God of the Oppressed,* chap. 8.

14. William Jones refers to Camus and Sartre and their formulation of the problem of evil. I think that is a mistake, because the problem can easily become an intellectual issue for seminar discussions rather than something to which we are called to fight against in this world. I find nothing in Jones's formulation of the problem of evil that would lead me to fight against it in this world.

9

Theology as Reflection Upon the Roots of Christian Culture

THOMAS J. J. ALTIZER

The overwhelming problem that defines the contemporary theological situation is the virtual dichotomy between church or religion and culture or the dominant currents of contemporary consciousness and society. While this problem is certainly not confined to Christianity, it is particularly acute therein, for not since its beginning has Christianity been so isolated from culture. It is in this situation that sectarian forms of Christianity flourish, just as this is the situation that has realized a chasm between church and university theology and a truly new chasm between thinking or consciousness and faith. This is also a perilous situation for Protestantism, for Protestantism has been allied with and an expression of a historical era which is now coming to an end, and as we fully and decisively enter a postmodern world it would appear that Protestantism must ever increasingly become identified with our past. If one can rejoice that a new or reborn Catholicism is being realized in our era, this is nevertheless a profoundly disconcerting situation for the non-Catholic theologian, and the question must now be confronted as to whether or not such a theologian continues to have a genuinely theological vocation.

Nothing is more important for the theologian who would confront this crisis than an awareness of its historical ground. Perhaps our closest historical analogue is the Dark Ages, a time when Christianity largely lost the synthesis which was effected between the Christian and the classical worlds in the patristic age but also a time when the Christian world was wholly insular and agrarian and thus was isolated from all other forms of culture and society. Even if the

Carolingian scribes succeeded in preserving the great bulk of what remains to us of Latin literature, the ancient classical world only actually entered the Carolingian world through the Roman Catholic Church, and the Catholic Church between the late sixth and the late eleventh century was innocent of all but the rudiments of classical culture. John Scotus Erigena does appear as a light shining in the darkness of the ninth century, but his writings were condemned and recondemned to destruction, and thereafter exercised only an underground and all but hidden influence. Medieval philosophy and theology as a living tradition is born only with Anselm of Canterbury, a birth which was a rebirth of Augustinian Neoplatonism, and the evolution of Christian medieval thinking remained at least two centuries behind its Islamic counterpart.

The truth is that Christianity had to be reinitiated into classical culture through Islam, and it was through Islam that Christianity was once again initiated into Greek *theoria,* an initiation issuing in the birth of an Aristotelian scholasticism which even yet has not come to an end. Nevertheless, an essential ground of medieval scholasticism was its integral and fundamental relation to the Gothic world as a whole, a world extending from a new imperial church to the birth of the European bourgeoisie in the new cities, and to the glories of Gothic art, architecture, and poetry. A Thomistic *analogia entis* is simply abstract and unreal apart from that world, and the disintegration of the Gothic world issued in the advent of nominalism, a nominalism dissolving and reversing every integral and coherent relation between reason and revelation, nature and grace, and time and eternity, and a nominalism that has perhaps only been fully realized in our own world.

But just as the theologian of the Dark Ages was largely ignorant of classical culture, so the theologian of today is ignorant of Christian culture, indeed, the theologian commonly proceeds as though such a culture had simply never existed. Despite the fact that our world has brought forth a vast body of critical studies of Dante, Milton, and Blake, studies re-creating their respective imaginative and historical worlds, these primal Christian epic poets are wholly ignored by virtually every theologian, and thereby is ignored all but an ecclesiastical Christian tradition, thereby positivistically reducing the Christian tradition to a sectarian history, a history of what is little more than a cult or sect. A newly primitive Protestant mind appears to believe that the Bible is meaningful and real apart from tradition, or apart from all but a purely ecclesiastical tradition, thereby perpetuating the fiction that the Christian tradition is simply an ecclesiastical tradition, a fiction most profoundly created by Karl Barth. The price of this fiction is, of course, the total isolation of Christianity from culture, and even the isolation of Christianity from Christian culture, for while Kierkegaard founded modern theology by establishing a negative dialectical relationship between faith and culture, Barth ended modern theology by embarking upon a *Church Dogmatics* in which a nonecclesiastical history and world is present only in its all too literal absence.

Barth's renunciation of his original Kierkegaardian discipleship is the paradigmatic move of twentieth-century Protestant theology; it decisively established what is now openly manifest as Protestant theology, and even Protestant thinking as such, for both Hans-Georg Gadamer and Paul Ricoeur are theologically Barthian, and it is its Barthian core which is the secret of the power of contemporary theological hermeneutics. Barthianism or pure neo-orthodoxy can be a theological vocation today, indeed, it is virtually the only visible one with power and authority, at least in the Protestant world. But it can only have power and authority in an ecclesiastical realm, in the world of the seminary and the church, a church and seminary world which is now almost wholly in retreat from the larger world about it, and is thus regressing to a sectarian identity. But that is the only identity which is possible for a neo-orthodox Christianity today, for here the "neo" is all-important, for it means at bottom a transhistorical or transcultural form of Christianity, a Christianity which has historically existed only in the world of the sects. Is it possible that the advent of a postmodern world can make possible a universal realization of a transhistorical and transcultural Christianity? This would appear to be the wager of almost all contemporary Protestant theologians.

Let us pose a contrary wager. Our historical and cultural world remains at bottom a Christian world, even if invisible as such to the Protestant if not the Catholic theologian, and it is Christian even in its deepest ground. While this might seem to be a simply paradoxical wager, it is not such if Hegelianism is recognized as the reigning philosophy of our world, even as Aristotelianism was of an earlier Christian world. For Hegel was a profoundly Christian thinker, even if a "heretical" thinker, and a recent major study of Hegel by Quentin Lauer maintains not only that Hegel is clearly the most "God-ine-briated" of all philosophers but that his concept of God is the most fundamental ground of his thinking as a whole. Kierkegaard, even as Marx, was a Hegelian thinker, even if, like Marx, a negative Hegelian thinker, and it is clear that Kierkegaard is the one openly Christian modern thinker who continues to have a deep impact upon modern thinking and culture as such. There is no more pathological sign of twentieth-century Protestant theology than its turn away from Kierkegaard, for that entails a turn away from the whole world of culture, a turn creating a vacuum necessitating the creation of a "nontheological" theological thinking. But it need not be only "non-theological," as witness the advent of modern Catholic theology, a theology eclipsing its twentieth-century Protestant counterparts in D. G. Leahy's *Novitas Mundi*. That this book is unknown in church and seminary today is simply a sign of Protestantism's retreat from culture, a retreat so great that the Protestant theological mind no longer even seeks a dialogue with culture, as witness the world of Protestant publications today.

Yet we cannot be open to our world as a Christian world if we are closed to a Christian history and world transcending its cultic expressions. For to recognize Hegelianism as a seminal power in our world is to recognize a Christian world transcending the confession and worship of the church, a Christian world that was once fully coincident with the fullness of Western culture, and a Christian world in which there was a full and integral synthesis or correlation between theology and culture. The Gothic world is obviously such a synthesis, and Giotto and Dante are manifestly profoundly Christian artists, and artists who were creators of a uniquely Western Christian culture. But so likewise is Milton such an artist, and a profoundly Protestant poet, for *Paradise Lost* is or should be to the Protestant mind what Dante's *Commedia* is to the Catholic mind, which is to say the epic source and foundation of the classical Protestant world. Moreover, Milton is the most fully theological of all our poets, or the most systematically so, for *Paradise Lost* was both preceded by and grounded in *De Doctrina Christiana*, Milton's own systematic theological treatise, a treatise that would appear to be wholly unknown in the Protestant theological world today.

Milton's *Christian Doctrine* could not be published in his own lifetime. He left it as a Latin manuscript of 745 numbered pages, and it was not published until 1825. No Protestant publisher has ever published this great work, and even today it is only available in volumes 14 to 17 of the *Columbia Milton*, although it will soon be available in the *Yale Milton*. Yet as both a Protestant and a biblical systematic theology, this work surely transcends Calvin's *Institutes*, and it may well be the most purely biblical systematic theology ever written. In the face of the *Christian Doctrine* and *Paradise Lost*, one is tempted to say that the Protestant Reformation did not truly or fully occur until the seventeenth century, and it is all too significant that these works are both reflections and embodiments of the English Revolution, which is to say that unique political revolution which inaugurated the revolutionary history of the West (Milton was Cromwell's Latin secretary and the great apologist for the English Revolution). Now what must be truly baffling to the contemporary theological mind is that *Christian Doctrine* and *Paradise Lost* are manifestly and integrally related to each other, so that the poem, as is now critically recognized, cannot be properly understood apart from the theological treatise, and it is the treatise which gives a full and decisive biblical warrant for most of the "heresies" of the poem, "heresies" that biblical scholars today commonly recognize as being biblical (e.g., mortalism and anti-Trinitarianism). While neither Luther nor Calvin dared to challenge the patristic dogmas of the church, and at this point as at so many others thereby remaining medieval Christians, Milton sought a fully and truly biblical faith, a faith which is embodied in *Paradise Lost*.

Paradise Lost is not only our greatest English epic poem but it is also our greatest modern epic, and thereby is a primal source and ground of modernity. To suggest that the satanic imagery and energy of this epic is later conceptually realized in Hegel's pure negativity is to suggest that *Paradise Lost* is, at least in part, to our world what the *Iliad* and the *Odyssey* were to the classical world. But this is to suggest that the modern world is grounded in a rebirth of the Bible itself, and not in its periphery but in its innermost foundations, foundations that lie at the center of modern consciousness and society. *Paradise Lost* is also an apocalyptic epic, as is now increasingly being recognized, but thereby it joins Dante's *Commedia* and Blake's *Milton* and *Jerusalem*, so that if we take these four epics together as our modern Christian epic, we can thereby see that the Western Christian imagination has been far more profoundly biblical than has the Western theological tradition as such. The *Commedia* is now being theologically unraveled, and Dante was not a Thomist, or not where it counted most, and certainly not in his vision of man, history, and society, for here he was more deeply and more fully biblical than the scholastic tradition has ever been. Likewise, *Milton* and *Jerusalem* are fully apocalyptic epics, and manifestly so. They unveil Jesus as an apocalyptic prophet, and a totally and purely apocalyptic prophet and center, and do so long before this discovery occurred in historical scholarship.

It is perhaps understandable that New Testament scholars should ignore Blake, as all of them do, although this becomes grotesque when embodied in New Testament scholars seeking a literary meaning of the Bible, but it is even more grotesque when systematic theologians ignore the whole Christian epic tradition, and do so even when seeking the meaning of humanity. Yet just as Hegel is our most "God-inebriated" philosopher, our Christian epic poets are our most "God-inebriated" poets, and each of them embodies both profoundly new and deeply biblical visions of God. And this is what is most unacceptable to the theologian: the very conjunction of the truly new and the truly biblical appears to be impossible to the theological mind, and doubly or triply impossible when it is integrally conjoined with a total vision of God, humanity, and the cosmos, as it always is in fully and genuinely epic poetry. Moreover, full epic poetry is by necessity revolutionary poetry, for it both envisions and embodies a truly new world, a world that is fully realized in the dynamic movements of both consciousness and society. Does the theologian dare to affirm that the Bible itself is newly realized and reborn in consciousness and society, and reborn so as to realize new and ever more universal worlds?

The theologian who makes the wager that is offered here must wholly reconceive the given and established identity of the vocation of theology, and particularly so insofar as theology is conceived as the servant of the church, and most particularly so when the church is given a wholly ecclesiastical or cultic identity. If theology is inconceivable apart from church, then let us recover the image of the invisible church, that mystical body of which Christ is the head, and which is universal in time and space (Milton's *Christian Doctrine*, chap. 24). This is a church that is fully correlative with a universal historical world, a world that was first conceived in the West by Dante, and first expressed in Dante's *De Monarchia*, his one open theological treatise, a theological treatise that made possible the *Commedia* even as Milton's *De Doctrina Christiana* made possible *Paradise Lost*. Indeed, Dante's articulation in the third part of this treatise of "the universal community of the human race" (*universalis civilitas humani generis*), or simply "the human community" (*humana civitas*), established for the first time in the West the ultimate ideal of a universal historical order and world. Dante thereby established a Christian poetic tradition that reaches a high point in Blake's vision of that "One Man" in *Jerusalem:*

> We live as One Man; for contracting our infinite senses
> We behold multitude, or expanding, we behold as one,
> As One Man all the Universal Family, and that One Man
> We call Jesus the Christ; and he in us, and we in him. . . .
> He is the Good Shepherd, he is the Lord and master,
> He is the Shepherd of Albion, he is all in all.

(38:17–24)

Blake's Albion is a symbolic figure who is a cosmic and universal divine humanity, a total humanity who is divine and cosmic at once, and who is ultimately realized as Jerusalem, the apocalyptic name and identity of Christ. If nothing else, Albion might be a symbolic figure for a new theologian, a theologian who is determined to uncover a universal destiny, and a destiny that has both occurred historically and is occurring even now. And a universal destiny is not simply a destiny that occurs in all human beings, it occurs universally throughout the society and consciousness, and occurs therein in the most dynamic and transfiguring moments and modes of consciousness and society, modes and moments which kenotically empty themselves so as to actualize and realize a universal humanity and world. Our epic tradition envisions this voyage and war as an apocalyptic process and reality, a process really and actually occurring within and about us, and occurring so as to realize what Blake names as Jerusalem, the very Jerusalem whom Blake discovered to be celebrated throughout the Bible, and the Jerusalem who is hidden and buried in what our fallen consciousness knows as religion and church.

Epilogue:
The Vitality of Theology

It is perilous indeed to attempt a summary of the variety of perspectives represented in this volume. This is all the more true if one is not only an observer but also an interested participant in (not to mention something of an instigator of) this discussion. Still more there is the risk of deflecting concern for the object of theology (however construed) to a typological interest in theology as an object.

Is it possible to speak of consensus in the midst of diversity? Perhaps the most significant consensus represented by these essays is the shared conviction that, however differently construed, theology is regarded as a possible, a significant, indeed a challenging and urgent task. It would be easy to dismiss this as special pleading. After all, theologians might be reasonably supposed to have a vested interest in maintaining the importance of their work. Yet anyone familiar with the last quarter century of theological discussion in North America will realize that it is by no means self-evident that theologians should exhibit such confidence concerning not only the importance but even the possibility of theological labor. We may be witnessing a dramatic change in the theological climate.

Yet it would appear that consensus scarcely reaches any farther, that there is an astonishing divergence in the ways in which theology is understood and practiced.

Consider the diversity. Kaufman directs our attention to the task of constructing the concept of God as a task which exceeds any particular religious tradition, while Wainwright insists that theology must take seriously the lived experience of the community of faith. While others insist on the importance of lived and shared experi-

143

ence, they point to a different community—the black community with its experience of God's liberating action (Cone) or the experience of women both within and without the life of established churches (Ruether). Míguez-Bonino points to a reflection upon the praxis of the community of faith in specifically economic and political spheres as the task of theology, while Altizer directs our attention to the resources of a wider culture whose artistic expressions reflect a biblical faith outside the confines of church and sect. Like Altizer, Gilkey is concerned with the "religious substance" of culture but conceives this not as the expression of biblical faith but as "world" to which the church must address itself. I speak of doctrine and its reformulation, while Cobb speaks of the Christian intellectual concerned to address whatever issues are of importance. Far many other divergences could be mentioned.

Yet apparently irreconcilable alternatives turn out on closer examination to be complementary or convergent. Two illustrations will suffice for many: Altizer seems to celebrate a Christian culture outside the church, while Míguez-Bonino emphasizes an unremittingly critical attitude toward the economic and political structures of this same culture. Yet an openness to Marxist economic analysis is really possible on the basis of a supposition that critical dimensions of biblical faith come to expression outside and against what is normally thought of as church. The "intellectualism" of Cobb or Kaufman might be opposed to the concern for liberating praxis manifest in Míguez-Bonino and Cone, yet on further inspection it becomes clear that they all share a concern for the critical function of theology over against self-absolutizing idols, structures, systems in both "church" and "world."

But just as apparent divergences yield unexpected convergence, so also apparent agreement may conceal tensions. For example, while Wainwright's emphasis upon the community of faith may appear to be like my own concern for doctrine, I do not think he would be happy with my emphasis upon the reconstruction or deconstruction of doctrine. Similar tensions and divergences may be discerned beneath the surface of other apparently convergent views.

Some may think of this shifting kaleidoscope of intersections and divergences as itself a sign of irremediable crisis in theology. How can this work be undertaken at all in the absence of a consensus concerning its aim and object, its sources, its center, its boundaries? The apparent force of this question points us toward an important feature of contemporary theology. For if we may speak of scholasticism as that view of theology which operates within and insists upon a well-established consensus concerning the aim and object of theology, then it is clear that the views represented here both individually and collectively insist upon a rupturing of this consensus and an opening of theological work in the direction of a vigorously contested (and celebrated) pluralism.

One may speak, then, of the freedom of theological work. Freedom from ecclesial preoccupation (Kaufman, Altizer), freedom from sterile academicism (Wainwright, Cone), freedom over against the structures of alienation (Míguez-Bonino, Gilkey, Ruether). And with this freedom comes also the renunciation of authoritarian claims for itself, a welcoming of divergence, a willingness and obligation to explain oneself to others of disparate views and to take seriously their objections and counterclaims. Underlying and motivating this freedom is the vocation of freedom, that is, the sense that theological work is by no means an end in itself but seeks instead to summon world and church and academy toward freedom. Pluralism in theology is the indispensable context for the exercise of theology as a liberating discipline.

This pluralism may be seen as mere relativism in which nothing remains but to transform theology into a historical and sociological analysis of this diversity. But for others this pluralism is itself a provocation to the responsible freedom of articulating and pursuing one's own vision of theological work in companionship with those of quite different views.

For myself I must say that I welcome this diversity, this dialogue, this opening. In whatever way we conceive the work of theology, each of us is aware of the partiality and provisionality of our own view and of the impossibility of undertaking this work alone and out of our own resources. None of us are bashful about putting forward our own views and defending them vigorously. But this comes not from absolutistic self-confidence about our own access to the truth but from a confident reliance upon those of divergent perspectives to correct and complement our own partial insights. And beyond this we may speak of a shared confidence in the illuminating and transforming power of truth and thus in the fruitfulness of that lifelong struggle to discern the truth which is the proper vocation of the theologian.

Index

Abelard, Peter, 79
Allmen, J.-J. von, 11, 19
Altizer, Thomas J. J., 144,
    145
Anselm, 81, 136
Aquinas, Thomas, 26, 27, 31,
    79, 81
Aristotle, 26
Athanasius, 80
Augustine, 26, 27, 80, 101,
    112, 122
Ayer, A. J., 49

Barfield, Owen, 82
Barth, Karl, 13, 15, 21, 56–
    57, 71, 81, 119, 122, 123,
    125, 127, 132 n. 1, 137
Basil, 80, 81
Baxter, Richard, 31
Berger, Peter, 22
Bernard of Clairvaux, 81
Blake, William, 136, 140,
    141–42
Boff, Clodovis, 43–44

Brown, Raymond, 11
Bultmann, Rudolf, 16, 123

Calvin, John, 79, 122, 139
Camus, Albert, 129, 130
Child, Brevard, 11
Clebsch, William A, 16
Cobb, John B., Jr., 144
Cone, James H., 144, 145
Congar, Yves, 12
Cozzens, James, 49
Crombie, I. M., 49

Daly, Mary, 28
Dante, 136, 138, 140, 141
Derrida, Jacques, 82

Ebeling, Gerhard, 24 n. 17
Edwards, Jonathan, 23
Erigena, John Scotus, 136

Fell, Margaret, 31
Ferre, Methold, 48 n. 3

George, Raymond, 11, 19
Gilkey, Langdon, 144, 145

Giotto, 138
Godamer, Hans-Georg, 137
Gramsci, Antonio, 48 n. 2
Gregory of Nyssa, 80
Gutiérrez, Gustavo, 131 n. 1

Harvey, Van A., 90
Hebblethwaite, Brian, 15
Hegel, Georg Wilhelm,
    137–38, 139, 140
Heidegger, Martin, 42
Heisenberg, Werner, 13
Hick, John H., 21
Hofstadter, Richard, 22

James, William, 58, 60
Jennings, Theodore W., 20
Jenson, Robert W., 24 n. 17
Jones, William, 129, 130, 133
    n. 12, 134 n. 14
Julian of Norwich, 31
Jüngel, Eberhard, 24 n. 17

Kasper, Walter, 12, 24 n. 17
Kaufman, Gordon D., 143,
    144, 145
Kierkegaard, Søren, 137, 138
King, Martin Luther, Jr., 130
Kühn, Ulrich, 12

Lash, Nicholas, 12
Lauer, Quentin, 138
Leahy, D. G., 138
Leenhardt, Franz J., 19
Lehman, K., 48 n. 3
Lévi-Strauss, Claude, 80
Luther, Martin, 27, 79, 112,
    139

Marx, Karl, 21, 138
Melancthon, Philipp, 83
Metz, J. B., 110
Míguez-Bonino, José, 144,
    145
Milton, John, 136, 138–40,
    141
Moltmann, Jürgen, 24 n. 17
Morris, Arnold, 10

Nasr, Seyyed Hossein, 23 n. 2
Niebuhr, H. Richard, 9, 59,
    110
Niebuhr, Reinhold, 87
Nilus of Ancyra, 24 n. 10
Nissiotis, Nikos, 19

Pannenberg, Wolfhart, 12,
    15, 24 n. 17

Rahner, Karl, 12, 24, n. 17
Ricoeur, Paul, 137
Ruether, Rosemary Radford,
    144, 145
Runyon, Theodore, 21
Russell, Letty, 124

Saliers, Donald E., 20
Sartre, Jean-Paul, 57, 129,
    130
Schillebeeckx, Edward, 12
Schleiermacher, Friedrich, 3,
    5, 8
Seils, Martin, 12
Spener, Philip J., 83
Steiner, George, 16–17

Tillard, Jean, 12
Tillich, Paul, 87, 90, 112, 119, 123, 127
Torrance, T. F., 13
Toulmin, Stephen, 13, 14
Tracy, David, 15, 23

Updike, John, 15

van Buren, Paul, 22
von Rad, Gerhard, 38

Wainwright, Geoffrey, 143, 144, 145
Waits, Jim L., 7
Wesley, John, 21, 79
Wilmore, Gayraud S., 132 nn. 1, 5
Whitehead, Alfred North, 118, 119